Dictionary of
North American Indians
and Other Indigenous Peoples

Text and illustrations by
Gilbert Legay

Design
Pierre Clavère

Photo credits
p. 38, 47, 63, 187: Bridgeman Giraudon
p. 71: Jeff Foott/Nature PL Hoa Qui
p. 121: Walter Bibikow/AGE Hoa Qui
p. 134: Pascale Beroujon/Hoa Qui
p. 176: Murray Lee/AGE Hoa Qui
p. 82, 148, 179, 189: Bibliothèque des Arts Décoratifs, Paris.
p. 7, 168, 200: DR

The wording of any text excerpted from another publication
may differ slightly due to its translation.

First edition for North America published 2007 by Barron's Educational Series, Inc.
Original edition copyright © 2005 by Casterman.
U.S. edition copyright © 2007 by Barron's Educational Series, Inc.

English translation by Corinne McKay

All inquiries should be addressed to:
Barron's Educational Series, Inc.
250 Wireless Boulevard
Hauppauge, New York 11788
www.barronseduc.com

ISBN-13: 978-0-7641-6043-1
ISBN-10: 0-7641-6043-5

Library of Congress Control No.: 2006936484

Printed in China

987654321

FOREWORD

H istorically, movies and comic strips have given us a stereotypical image of the North American Indian, an image that has little in common with the variety of cultures and ways of life of the inhabitants of this vast continent. For example, in stories that showed the bravery of the pioneers or the rage of the "blue coats," Indians were rarely the heroes. They were portrayed as cruel and aggressive, with a sense of honor and contempt for death, which made them dangerous. This unfair simplification led to additional assumptions about their ways of life: All Indians hunted buffalo on fast wild mustangs, slept in tipis, and danced screaming around tall, carved totem poles. Although this picture approximated the general image of the Indians living on the Great Plains, buffalo were not found everywhere on the continent, types of dwellings varied from east to west and

from north to south, and big totem poles belonged to the culture of the fishing peoples on the northwest coast. In reality, there were as many differences between a whale-killing Nootka on the Pacific coast, a buffalo-hunting Pawnee, and a Creek farmer in the Alabama valley as there are in Europe (if we can use a few stereotypes) between a Norwegian sailor, an Austrian military officer, and a vineyard owner in Tuscany: differences in environment, language, lifestyles, among others. Given these varied cultures, which deserve a better understanding, it is worthwhile and interesting to broaden our familiarity with the extraordinary dimensions of these peoples which we've named Indians or American Indians, taken from the name of a land that was not theirs (the Indies) or an explorer (Amerigo Vespucci) who was not the first one to discover them.

3

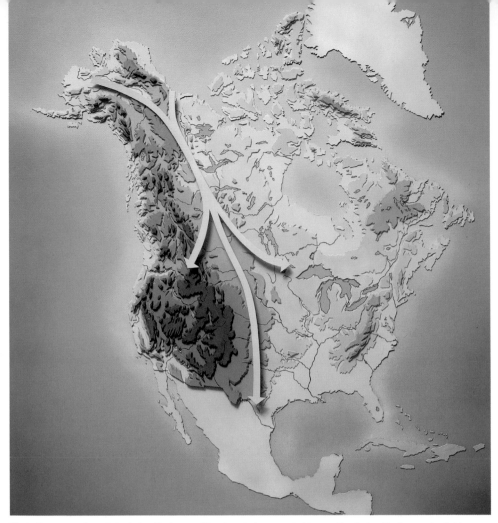

The Indians came from Asia during the ice age. They traveled across what is now the Bering Strait on an ice bridge. After that, they spread across the entire continent.

Let the Adventure Begin!

Like all humans, the Indian peoples have their roots in Africa and the gradual migrations that *Homo sapiens* undertook as the Earth cooled and warmed. When the ice mass increased, the water levels lowered and the connections between the continents (Bering, Panama, etc.) emerged completely, creating natural bridges that animals used, with the hunters following right behind them! This is how some of them went from Siberia to Alaska during two partic-

ularly favorable periods (40,000–30,000 and 25,000–10,000 B.C.). The entry corridors were the Mackenzie valley in the north, and the Yukon valley across Alaska. Traveling on hazardous, ice-covered paths, on the trail of the animals they were following, humans were irresistibly drawn south. Before them spread an immense country where nature was bountiful. The lakes and rivers were filled with fish, and the deep and varied forests alternated with plains rich in abundant game. For thousands of years, generation after generation, the future "Indians" moved forward, occupying North America, and then Central and South America. Carbon 14 testing has allowed us to detect traces of human presence as far back as 12,000 B.C. in Patagonia, a distant region located more than 11,000 miles from the Bering Strait. This was quite a feat for the oldest waves of migration, people who traveled at a rate of one-half to one mile per year! Other tests performed using the same technique also confirm this progression from north to south: 23,000 years to Mexico, between 17,000 and 32,000 years to Brazil, and 24,000 to 25,000 years to Peru. Fate has a way of working things out. Conditions were ripe for a unique experience in the history of the human race. Everything happened as if a higher power, a sort of Great Spirit, like a researcher in his cosmic laboratory, had decided to change the scheduled program, isolating a part of humanity, allowing it to develop completely alone, with total self-sufficiency.

Getting to Know Each Other

We know that this isolation lasted until October 1492, when Christopher Columbus, sent by the rulers of Spain, dropped anchor off the coast of Guanahani, an island in the Bahamas now known as San Salvador. Columbus, a navigator from Genoa, Italy, was convinced that he had reached the far coast of Asia, and named these lands "West Indies." Naturally, he also called their inhabitants Indians. After this discovery, and before any mention was made of a new continent, many people throughout the sixteenth century

thought that this was a narrow strip of land that would be easy to cross, and that on the other side was another ocean reaching the East Indies. Vasco de Balboa's mission reinforced this preconceived notion. In 1513, after learning from the local Indians that there was a vast body of water beyond the forests and the mountain ridges, Balboa crossed the isthmus of Panama and after walking for ten days, discovered the Pacific ocean on September 25. But something else caught everyone's attention: the fact that this new land was inhabited by humans defied all logic. To sixteenth-century Europeans, this posed a question as disturbing as if today we discovered the presence of humans on an unknown planet.

The first colonists, referring to the Bible, took the Indians to be the descendants of Japheth, the third son of Noah. Until the eighteenth century, scholars advanced various hypotheses to explain these people's presence: they could only be the descendants of people who escaped from a cataclysmic event: the disappearance of Atlantis, the fall of Carthage, the diaspora of the tribes of Israel, and so on. Linguists found similarities between their dialects and certain ancient languages: among them Hittite, Phoenician, and Celtic. But historical and linguistic speculations were of little interest to the Spanish, who sent their captains to attack the native people and make new conquests. Having entered the new continent through the Antilles, the Spanish set up their bases in Cuba and Santo Domingo. From there, they expanded their conquest to Panama, Mexico, Peru, Chile, Argentina, and Paraguay.

The Call of the North

So, exploration to the north seemed much less promising to them. To quench their thirst for gold and riches, many of them nevertheless chased their dreams on the mysterious lands of the Indians north of the Gulf of Mexico. From Ponce de Léon (1513) to Pamfilo de Narvaez (1528), from the expedition of de Soto (1539) to that of Coronado (1540), the Spanish efforts were nothing but a somber litany of pillages, nameless atrocities, and gratuitous killings. To the conquistadors' foolish boldness and cruelty, the Indians responded with indomitable and untamed determination. However, the first contact wasn't always negative. The tribes of the Mississippi basin were naturally distrustful, but those in the Southeast proved themselves to be welcoming, at least when they weren't aware of the Spaniards' detestable reputation. However, Spanish swords came out of their scabbards, and the killing began. In the face of the least bit of resistance, the Spanish could only envision a strategy of fists, fire, and terror. Only one of them understood that it might have been possible to act differently in everyone's best interest. His name was Nuñez Cabeza de Vaca. After surviving Narvaez's expedition, he wandered for more than seven years among the tribes in Texas, and realized that it was possible to get along with and live with the Indians, as long as one respected them and didn't try to threaten their freedom.

In their contacts with the French and the English, the story of the Indians in the Northeast was very different. Quickly, these two powers became engaged in a fight on the same continent for worldwide domination, most of which unfolded in Europe and on the seas. The Indian tribes supplied large battalions of combat units, without concerning themselves with the stakes. The Indians were understandably obsessed with safeguarding their independence and their territory, and thus with the short-term objective of choosing the most acceptable of these two powers. Almost all of the tribes opted for France over the English, with the notable and important exception of the Iroquois.

The Journey Westward

When, in 1783 at the end of the two wars, the British soldiers were forced to yield to the pugnacious men of the United States, the tribes found themselves faced with a new state whose future depended on westward expansion.

Since Columbus first set foot on San Salvador, there were 350 years of conflict and a few peace treaties, some encouraging first meetings, and a few lasting alliances, but also a lack of understanding, distrust, betrayals, killings, and unbearable cruelties. How many Indians were on the entire North American continent at the time of Christopher Columbus' discovery? We can only estimate: Some will say one million; others will say ten million. If we take an average of four million, for a continent of more than 12.5 million square miles (the United States plus Canada), the average is one person for every three square miles. Four centuries later, the people that the first white men called Redskins (fooled by the color that they painted their faces and torsos), these brave and courageous warriors who had been penned up in reservations, numbered no more than 285,000. Discovering peoples, cultures, and beliefs, the European and Christian invaders were strong in status and weapons. They could have advanced peacefully, made use of their curiosity, created brotherly ties, examined their customs, and benefited from their knowledge . . . but none of this happened! Only the law of swords and fire was applied by men of violence, obsessed by the lure of riches and the possession of lands.

Which Path?

In the last hundred years, the Indian population has quintupled, and in 1990, more than half of them lived in cities. This proportion of city-dwelling Indians has since continued to grow consistently. Certain tribes have profited from the underground riches of their reservation, from sumptuous landscapes that draw tourists, or from favorable legislation related to gaming facilities. Others, and these are more numerous, stagnate without much to do, worn down by unemployment and alcoholism. According to John Collier, the commissioner of the Bureau of Indian Affairs and a well-known defender of the tribes in the 1930s, the Indians may have been spared the effects of the industrial revolution thanks to "their passion for the human person, combined with their passion for the land and its webs of life." They may thus have become symbols of the fight to be carried on in the face of threats such as industrial and nuclear pollution, for the respect of peoples and cultures, and for the simple right to difference.

In concluding his preface to our *Atlas of North American Indians* (1993), Philippe Jacquin wrote, "In the movie *Dances with Wolves*, the Sioux shaman Kicking Bird, happy to be able to converse with lieutenant John Dunbar, who has become a Sioux and is happy for their friendship, confides in him: 'Which path YOU and ME.' These few words condense all of the difficulty that humans have in understanding each other, and that cultures have in listening to each other."

In the face of the threats that weigh on the planet and its inhabitants, it is useful to ask ourselves, "Which path for THEM and for US?"

Gilbert Legay

THE INDIAN LANDS

Anthropologists have divided the North American continent into ten regions, each corresponding to an ecosystem. In each region, the Indians of various tribes shared essentially the same living conditions, both in terms of climate and in terms of the characteristics and plant and animal resources of their environment.

The Arctic

The Arctic is an extremely cold zone that extends from Labrador to the southern coasts of Alaska. The region is very inhospitable and practically devoid of vegetation (some mosses, lichens, etc.), and it requires humans to use extreme ingenuity and perseverance to survive. The Inuits' only food resources were marine mammals (seals, walrus, cetaceans, etc.), fish, and some birds in summer. The Inuits spoke Eskimo-Aleut; they were nomadic in summer, seeking the best place to subsist, and were sedentary in winter.

The Subarctic

The Subarctic is the vast region (almost 2,000,000 square miles or 3,200,000 square kilometers) that occupies the majority of Canada and the Alaskan interior. The western part is a zone of mountains and tundra, covered with snow for most of the year. South and east of the Subarctic are lands of taiga (boreal forests of silver birch, aspen, and conifers), crisscrossed by rivers and dotted with many lakes. Mosses and blueberry bushes form the underbrush. The climate is very harsh, with very long winters when the days are short and snowfalls are abundant. The summer is mild, but because of mosquitoes, people must cover themselves up and travel to areas that are less populated by insects. Caribou is the primary food source, along with fish and small game. The western half was inhabited by Athabascan-speaking tribes (as well as Beaver, Chipewyan, Dogrib, Kutchin, etc.), and the east by Algonquian-speaking tribes such as Cree, Montagnais, and Naskapi.

Woodlands

The Woodlands region was bounded on the north by the Saint Lawrence Valley and the Great Lakes region, and from the east to the south by the Mississippi and Ohio Valleys as far as the Atlantic coast. It represented one-fifth of the present-day United States, and was covered with a thick forest, of which only one one-hundredth remains! The ground was fertile, the water was abundant, and the flora and fauna supplied all of the resources that the Indians needed. The people were hunters, fishermen, and farmers (mainly corn) and from this immense forest, they drew the materials necessary for producing weapons and household utensils and for building dwellings and protective barriers around villages. The region was divided between the Algonquian (Fox, Sauk, Menominee, Shawnee, Powhatan, Ojibwa, etc.) and Iroquoian (Huron, Iroquois, etc.) languages.

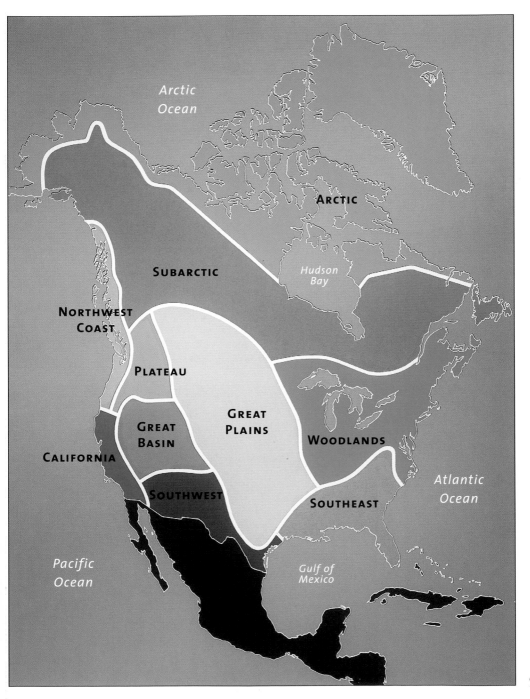

Arctic
Ocean

ARCTIC

SUBARCTIC

Hudson
Bay

NORTHWEST
COAST

PLATEAU

GREAT
PLAINS

GREAT
BASIN

WOODLANDS

CALIFORNIA

SOUTHWEST

SOUTHEAST

Atlantic
Ocean

Pacific
Ocean

Gulf of
Mexico

9

The Southeast

The hot and humid region South of the Woodlands, including the Appalachian Mountains, Florida, and the coast of the Gulf of Mexico, enjoys a favorable environment. The low-lying lands, criss-crossed by winding streams and rivers and bathed by the Mississippi Delta, receive alluvial deposits that make the soil extremely fertile. Vast swamps full of cypress trees and reeds complete the scene. There, the Indians were sedentary and grew corn, squash, and sunflowers. They could also hunt the abundant game and the fish living in the rivers. The main tribes of these inviting zones spoke Muskogan (Calusa, Chickasaw, Chocktaw, Creek, Timuca, etc.) with some pockets of Algonquian, Siouan (Catawba, Yuchi, etc.) and Iroquoian (Cherokee) speakers.

The Great Plains

In the heart of the North American continent, the Great Plains extended from southern Canada to the Gulf of Mexico, and from east to west from the Mississippi Valley to the Rocky Mountains. Some tribes were sedentary and grew corn, but most were nomads and traveled in their immediate area, depending on the passage of herds of bison through the immense grassy plains. Like the caribou for the Indians of the Subarctic, bison fulfilled all of the hunters' needs: food as well as other materials that were necessary for the life of the community (skins and furs, horns and bones, nerves and fat). The climate was continental (extreme cold from December to March, floods in the spring during the snow melt, and long, dry, and sometimes stiflingly hot summers) and the majority of the tribes

(Assiniboin, Crow, Dakota, Iowa, Mandan, Osage, Ponca, etc.) were Siouan language speakers. But the Great Plains were also crossed in all directions by tribes speaking Algonquian (Arapaho, Atsina, Blackfeet, Cheyenne, etc.), Caddoan, and Shoshonean (Comanche); the Kiowa formed a linguistic isolate.

The Southwest

The Southwest region includes the present-day states of Arizona and New Mexico and the southern part of Texas, to the Gulf of Mexico. A land of contrasts, this region offers the traveler a grandiose spectacle, alternating with canyons, deserts, mountains, cliffs made of truncated columns, plateaus placed on the sand-like immense overturned barges, and mesas. Throughout the region, the landforms limit the human horizon. A landscape is brushed in warm colors where all the shades of brown, ocher, red, and yellow combine, and all rest beneath an eternally blue sky. The climate is one of extremes, cold at night, oppressively hot during the day, dry and arid in summer, icy and snowy in winter. Sometimes, a violent thunderstorm breaks, transforming the dry riverbeds called *arroyos* into muddy torrents. The desert changes quickly and is adorned with millions of flowers that were waiting for the rain. The tribes are nomadic (Apache) or sedentary (Navajo and Pueblo), and speak the Athabascan, Shoshonean (Hopi), or Hokan (Yuma) languages. Small game and corn are their primary food resources.

California

California extends from north to south, from the Canadian border to the Mexican border, and from the Rocky Mountains in the east to the Pacific coast in the west. The climate is temperate and pleasant, and the Indians benefited from abundant sources of food. The tribes (Hupa, Miwok, Mojave, Pomo, Yurok, etc.) were peaceful for the most part, undoubtedly won over by the mild climate. There was a wide range of languages, but this did not generate misunderstandings. In the summer, people lived almost naked or covered with a simple loincloth. During the short winter, people wore long coats of animal skin and, for their infrequent travels, moccasins.

The Great Basin

The Great Basin included all of Nevada and Utah and large parts of Idaho, Wyoming, and Colorado. It is undoubtedly the least hospitable and poorest region: in its center, the Colorado River carved immense canyons dotted with bushes; to the north and east, the Snake and Green Rivers criss-cross vast prairies; the mountainous areas are covered with thick conifer forests. The Shoshonean-language Indians (Bannock, Shoshone, Paiute, Ute, Washo, etc.) devoted the bulk of their time to the search for food: roots, insects, lizards, small rodents, and birds stopping in swamps and ponds on their northward migration. In the summer, the Indians climbed to higher altitudes to gather pine kernel cones. The proximity of water lent itself to catching a maximum number of fish, which, once cleaned and dried, became reserves for difficult days.

The Plateau

A way point between the north and south and a true enclave between the Pacific coast and the Great Plains, the Plateau region offers a sumptuous and varied landscape: wooded mountains, deep valleys, bottomless canyons, rivers where flat water alternates with whitewater, and immense prairies of grasses and scrub. This was a zone of commercial transactions for the Salishan, Shahaptian, Algonquian, and Athabascan language tribes (notably the Nez Perce, Palouse, Salish, Thompson, Walla Walla, and Yakima). This mosaic of cultures, some of them influenced by the very structured societies of the coast, others having adopted the way of life of the Plains Indians, came together in a common activity: fishing for salmon in the network of the Columbia and Fraser Rivers and their tributaries.

The Northwest Coast

A narrow ribbon of land extending along the entire Pacific coast between California and Alaska (about 1,500 miles or 2,400 kilometers from north to south), lined with an almost continuous barrier of high coastal mountains, this region benefited from a temperate climate. The winds of the Pacific offered relatively mild weather as compared to that of the interior areas, but it was also very humid and rainy. The vegetation was luxurious: forests of giant conifers covered the major part of the territory. The tribes drew the bulk of their food resources from the ocean (tuna, herring, cetaceans, seals, dolphins, etc.). Although the Salishan dialects were dominant (Kwakiutl, Makah, Nootka, Tsimshian, etc.), many linguistic isolates of the major tribes (Haida, Tlingit, etc.) still pose the mysterious question of the origins of these people with their very particular cultures.

11

INDIAN LANGUAGES

Since the beginning of the nineteenth century, Americans have tried to establish names for Indian tribes and languages. The idea of a tribe did not mean the same thing for whites as it did for the Indians themselves: a tribe that seemed to constitute a well-defined entity was in fact a combination of two or three tribes, meaning that it was a confederation. On the contrary, many names that seem to designate different tribes actually related to a single group of Indians. The same uncertainty applied to preparing a list of Indian languages, which was an even more difficult task as it related to languages that were spoken and not written. These were very different one from the other, as is the case with Greek and English or Portuguese and Swedish.

Languages and Dialects

Within a linguistic family, the Indians could have great difficulty in communicating, and these difficulties were sometimes aggravated by cultural differences. This patchwork was the result of successive migrations of nomadic people who lived in small autonomous groups, each one defining its own cultural and linguistic identity over time. Around 1840, about fifty main languages had been identified, with each one including many languages or dialects. Since then, these estimates have been refined: we think that at least 500 languages were in use by the North American Indians when the whites arrived, and 221 languages have been identified and grouped into seventy-three main languages. In order to be included in a group, languages must show significant similarities, both in terms of vocabulary and in their grammatical structure, such that we believe that they came from the same main language. Similarities between the characteristics of many main languages defined in this way allow linguists to go back even further in time and envision a common root that is many thousands of years older.

From Asia to the New World

This research is obviously difficult and uncertain. Similarities with Asian languages, which have themselves evolved over time are at the limit of possibility. One exception concerns the Eskimo-Aleut language, which specialists see as being related to the Chukotian language of Northeast Siberia. Of the seventy-three main languages, thirty-one are what linguists call "isolates," meaning that they are spoken by only one human group. The forty-two others all include many languages or dialects. Work completed up until now has led to the identification of twelve linguistic families and many isolates on the North American continent.

Linguistic Families
(Situation at the Beginning of the Seventeenth Century)

• Eskimo-Aleut
The result of numerous dialects, this linguistic family is that of the peoples who live near the Arctic Circle and the Aleutian Islands and from the coasts of Alaska to the eastern coast of Labrador.

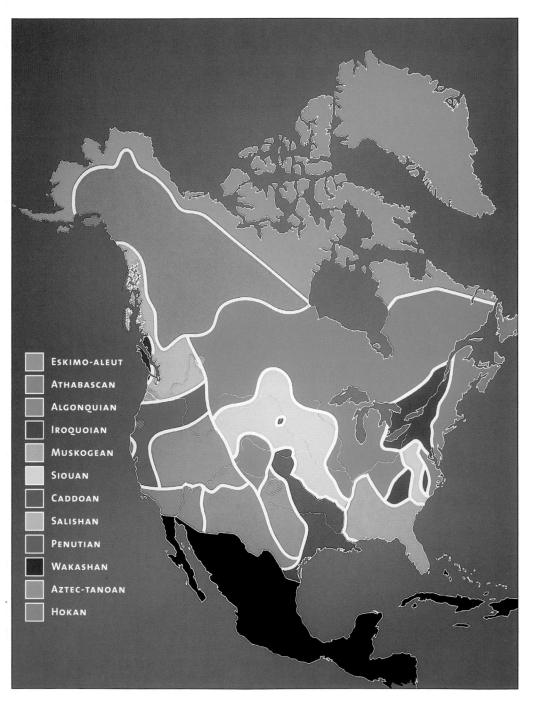

ESKIMO-ALEUT
ATHABASCAN
ALGONQUIAN
IROQUOIAN
MUSKOGEAN
SIOUAN
CADDOAN
SALISHAN
PENUTIAN
WAKASHAN
AZTEC-TANOAN
HOKAN

13

• Athabascan
(or Athapascan)

The Athabascan family includes the vast majority of the tribes of western Canada, from the Arctic Circle to the Saskatchewan River, some tribes of the Pacific coast (including the Hupa), and an important pocket in the American Southwest (Navajos and all the Apache groups: Chiricahua, Mescalero, Jicarilla, and Lipan).

• Algonquian

The Algonquian family includes almost twenty distinct languages, from Labrador to the Great Lakes (the Naskahi, Ottowa, Sauk, and Fox tribes), from the Great Lakes to the Rocky Mountains (Cree, Ojibwa, Blackfoot), and from the Hudson Bay to the Ohio Valley (Illinois, Shawnee). There are some additions to this primary zone: the region of the Atlantic coast bounded by the Saint Lawrence estuary and the Chesapeake Bay (the Micmac, Mahican, and Delaware tribes), then an enclave in the central Great Plains between the Platte and Arkansas Rivers, including part of the states of Wyoming, Colorado, Nebraska, and Kansas (Cheyenne, Arapaho).

• Iroquoian

The Iroquoian languages are spoken by the tribes of the Iroquois confederation (Cayuga, Oneida, Onondaga, Seneca, and Mohawk to the East of the Great Lakes region), the Huron (north of Lake Erie), the Tuscarora (coast of North Carolina), and the Cherokee (Tennessee). These languages were sometimes very different, at the limit of understanding even for other members of this same linguistic family. A relationship between Iroquoian on the one hand and Siouan and Caddoan on the other is defended by many linguists.

• Muskogean

The Muskogean family includes the languages of the peoples of the American Southwest. A disputed theory links Muskogean and Algonquian.

• Siouan

The tribes of the Siouan linguistic family seem to have come from the Great Lakes region around the eighteenth century to populate the Plains (Dakota, Assiniboin, Osage, Iowa, Mandan, and Crow tribes). Did they share the same territories as the Iroquois before this period? This would confirm the theory of the Siouan–Iroquoian relationship. This might also be suggested by the proximity of Siouan (Yuchi and Catawba) and Iroquoian (Tuscarora) enclaves.

• Caddoan

The Caddoan linguistic family includes the Caddo, Wichita, Pawnee and Arikara tribes. Certain specialists consider this to be a branch of Siouan.

• Salishan

The Salishan language family is located in a zone including the southern part of British Columbia and the American states of Washington, Idaho, and Montana. According to certain linguists, Salishan is related to Algonquian, but according to others, it is related to Wakashan.

• Penutian

According to linguists, the Penutian language family has variable boundaries. It includes tribes in California (Maidu, Miwok, Wintun, and Yokut) and the Shahaptian branch (Nez Perce, Cayuse).

• Wakashan

The Wakashan language family is located near Vancouver Island (Nootka and Makah tribes) and more to the north on the coast (Kwakiutl and Bella Bella). It has an unproven link with Algonquian.

• Aztec-Tanoan

The Aztec-Tanoan language family includes the Shoshonean branch (Shoshone, Ute, Paiute, Bannock, and Comanche) of the Great Basin and the Tanoan branch (Pima, Papago, Hopi, Acoma, Taos).

• Hokan

The Hokan language family in the American Southwest includes, within California and Arizona, the Mojave, Pomo, Chumash, Havasupai, Karok, and Yuma tribes, and, more to the north, the Washo tribe.

Many isolates should be added to this list. None of the theories aiming to link one or the other of these languages to the Athabascan, Algonquian, or Penutian families has rallied the majority of linguists.
Haida, **Tlingit**, and **Tsimshian** are all three located on the Pacific North coast.
Kootenai is located in the Southeast of British Columbia.

Kiowan is inside Texas.
Weitspekan of the Yurok is a language that some people associate with Algonquian.
Yukian is specific to the Yuki tribe and some satellite communities.
Karankawan and **Coathuiltecan** is associated with the Karankawa and Tonkawa tribes.
Lutuamian is spoken in the Klamath and Modoc tribes, which certain specialists associate with Penutian.
Chimakuan is specific to the Quileute tribe; specialists consider it to be an intermediary between Salishan and Wakashan.

Unfortunately, this list no longer corresponds to the current situation. In the past three centuries, numerous dialects and languages have disappeared, and others that are still spoken are threatened. For more than five centuries, the Great Plains were crossed in all directions by nomadic tribes. They belonged to seven linguistic families (Athabascan, Algonquian, Penutian, Siouan, Caddoan, Shoshonean, and Kiowan). So, these tribes had great difficulty communicating between themselves when their intentions were something other than warfare. The answer was the development of a sign language, a sort of "gesture Esperanto," which made it possible to share information or do business. Thus, Apache, Blackfeet, Nez Perce, Crow, Pawnee, Bannock, Kiowa, and others were able to exchange things other than arrows or tomahawk blows. This method of communication was practiced with great speed, with signs flowing together, one after the other. First trappers then soldiers became familiar with this language, which was an indispensable method for some to develop a trade in skins and for others to establish relationships of trust. But did they use it enough?

A

Abenaki

- From *Wabanaki*, "people from the dawn land."
- Language: Algonquian.
- Inhabited the northern part of the present-day state of Maine.
- Hunters and fishermen.
- People of simple customs, courageous, renowned warriors, the Abenaki formed a confederation of TRIBES. They were converted to Christianity by the Jesuits during the seventeenth century.
- Allies of the French, they carried out an intense war against the English. The English took revenge by massacring the Abenaki community founded by Father Sebastien Rôle in Norridgewock (1724).
- Weakened by battles and SMALLPOX, the Abenaki laid down their weapons in 1754. Seven hundred of them then fought alongside the Americans during the War of Independence.
- A very few descendants live in Quebec, Maine, and Vermont.

Acosta
José de (1540-1599)

The Provincial of the Spanish Jesuits in Peru. He wrote the *Natural and Moral History of the Indies* and was the first to put forth the theory that the Indians migrated into the American continent not by sea but by a piece of land that linked the Northwest of the continent with Asia.

Adena (people)

The people who settled 2,500 years ago in the Ohio River Valley, near the present-day city of Cincinnati. Where did they come from? The mystery remains unsolved, since their taller stature and more robust builds, proven by skeletons found by archaeologists, seem to differentiate them from their contemporaries and neighbors. Some scientists think that they came from Central America; others opt for the theory that they came down from the north. The Adena were farmers and distinguished themselves through a very elaborate worship of the dead, placing multiple objects and jewels in tombs. Large mounds (the source of the Adena people's nickname *Mound Builders*) were erected in the form of

animals such as snakes, birds, and turtles. The mounds were not group
tombs, but monuments associated with
funerary rituals with meanings that are
still a mystery. The largest is the *Great
Serpent Mound* near Cincinnati, which
measures 1,312 feet (400 meters) in
length.

Adobe

From the Arabic word for brick, *At-töb*,
which became *adobar* in Spanish. Brick
made of a mix of earth and dried plant
matter, molded in a wooden frame and
baked in the sun. These adobes were
used in the buildings of the peoples of
the Southwest, in particular the HOPI.

Agriculture

Numerous tribes were nomadic and
practiced only HUNTING, FISHING, and
gathering. Only sedentary or semi-
nomadic tribes devoted themselves to
agriculture: corn, squash, beans, potatoes, tomatoes, and also tobacco, which
was used as an accompaniment to various ceremonies and rituals.
• All of the tribes that occupied the
eastern third of the current United
States practiced agriculture, from the
Great Lakes region in the North to the
coast of the Gulf of Mexico in the south:
Iroquois, Huron, Delaware, Cherokee,
Chickasaw, Choctaw, Creek, among
others. The Indians fertilized their
fields by cutting down trees and
burning them. (This technique is

identical to the European practice of
clear cutting.)
• Some semi-nomadic tribes of the
Great Plains simultaneously engaged
in BISON hunting and growing corn.
• The tribes of the arid deserts of the
Southwest made up for scarcity of their
resources through rudimentary agriculture: Hopi, Navajo, Yuma, Zuni,
Havasupai, among others.
The ancestors of the
Papago and Pima had,
until the thirteenth
century, developed
very sophisticated irrigation techniques (*see* Hohokam).

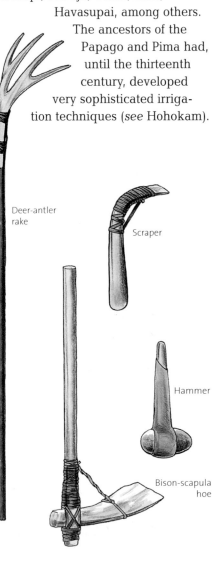

Deer-antler
rake

Scraper

Hammer

Bison-scapula
hoe

Ahtena

- Name means "Ice people."
- Language: Athabascan.
- Settled around the Copper River basin.
- The mouth of the Copper was discovered in 1781 by the Russian Nagaieff. Subsequent Russian expeditions encountered the Ahtena's hostility, and many ended in tragedy (Samoylof in 1796, Lastochkin in 1798, Klimoffsky in 1819, Gregorieff in 1844, Serebrannikof in 1848). After Alaska was purchased by the United States in 1882, other attempts (Abercrombie in 1884 and Allen in 1885) marked the beginning of peaceful relations.

Aleut

- Name of uncertain origin. May come from the word *aliat* (island) in the dialect of the Chuckchi of Kamchatka.
- Language divided into the *Atka* and *Unalaska* dialects. A variant of the *Eskimo-Aleut* linguistic group, like all of the Inuit people from Alaska to Greenland.
- Lived in the Aleutian islands on the Southwest coast of Alaska.
- Known since the expeditions of Bering in 1741 and Nerodchikof in 1745, the Aleut had to suffer the aggressions and exploitation of white traffickers. Their numbers declined dangerously until Alaska was purchased by the United States.

Algonquian

See Languages, pg. 14.

Algonquin

- Their name, derived from the Malecite *Elakomkwik* dialect, means "They are our allies." Another interpretation places the origin of the name in the Micmac language word *Algoomeaking*, "They harpoon fish." Champlain called them *Algoumequin* and the Iroquois called them *Adirondacks*, "Tree eaters."
- Algonquian language, to which they gave their name.
- Inhabited the land north of the Saint Lawrence, the area around Lake Huron to the east of Montreal, and both banks of the Ottawa River.

- Connected to the Chippewa, of whom they were the Eastern division (*see* Ojibwa).
- Lived in bands of a few hundred people, which were divided into hunting groups. The Algonquin also fished and farmed beans and corn. They lived in large wooden houses covered with silver birch bark.
- Faithful allies of the French after their meeting with CHAMPLAIN (1603). The Algonquin carried on a permanent war against the IROQUOIS.
- Between 4,000 and 5,000 Algonquin live today in eastern Ontario and western Quebec.

Alligator

(Alligater mississipiensis).
Sometimes as much as 19 feet (6 meters) long, the alligator is the largest reptile in North America. Its habitat extends from the coast of North Carolina to the coastal plain of South Texas, and particularly in the Florida EVERGLADES and at

the mouth of the Mississippi. Alligators are also called caymans (from the Caribbean word *acayonman*). The alligator is disappearing and is now protected by federal regulations, which ensure the survival of the species. The Indians in these regions aren't afraid of confronting alligators. The American crocodile (*Crocodylus acutus)* inhabits far southern Florida. It is no longer than 13 feet (4 meters) and is dark green in color, while the alligator is almost black.

Altar

This is one of the symbols of American Indian spirituality, and has been present since before their history was recorded. An altar may be a simple pile of rocks near a spring, or may be in a specially dug out spot, near a tree, or anywhere that SPIRITS are meant to live or appear. An altar may also be a place for sacrifices or offerings, a simple stone inside a *tipi* where the Indian will burn dried prairie grasses. For the HOPI, an altar is a complex group of symbolic objects: wooden sculptures representing spirits, masks, pipes, gourds, instruments used for ceremonies, rattles, whistles, ears of corn, etc., with the entire structure asking for rain and an abundant harvest.

Amherst
Baron Jeffrey (1717-1797)

An English marshal, named by William Pitt to be the head of the army sent to Canada in 1758. Amherst largely owed his first successes to the experience and energy of his lieutenants, James Wolfe and William Johnson. After the war against the French, Amherst was held in check by the Indians, whom he distrusted and hated. He had the unfortunate idea of having blankets contaminated with SMALLPOX distributed to the native peoples, which launched a genocidal technique that claimed thousands of lives.

Anasazi

Around 1000 B.C., they occupied a vast region called the Four Corners, since its geographic center was the point where the current states of Utah, Colorado, Arizona, and New Mexico meet. The Anasazi were first hunters and then farmers, but then became sedentary and built their wood-frame houses on MESAS. Their building techniques progressively evolved, and they perfected a type of adobe-based dwelling. At their height in the thirteenth century, they built troglodyte villages onto the sides of cliffs (Mesa Verde, Chelly Canyon). The choice of these types of sites was undoubtedly inspired by the Anasazi's concern for sheltering themselves from attacks. The women took care of the houses or worked on POTTERY and BASKET WEAVING. The men hunted, worked in the fields, or met in the KIVA to weave or talk amongst themselves. The Anasazi lived according to the rhythm of the seasons and various ceremonies which were required by their relationships with the KACHINAS. The kachinas were very powerful spirits, and the Anasazi wanted to win their favor.

Apache

- From *Apachu*, a Zuni word meaning "enemy." The Apache called themselves *Inde* or *Tinneh*, meaning "people."
- Language: Athabascan.
- Populated Arizona, Colorado, and New Mexico in two Apache groups: to the East, the Lipan Apache, Jicarilla (meaning "little basket") Apache, the Mescalero (meaning "mescal people"), and the Kiowa Apache; to the West, the Chiricahua Apache (meaning "mountain"), the Tonto Apache, the Western Apache, and the White Mountain Apache.
- The Apache were a heterogeneous group, with each tribe differentiating itself by its geographical location and the influence of its neighbors. Thus, the eastern Apache were influenced by the Plains Indians. The Apache were

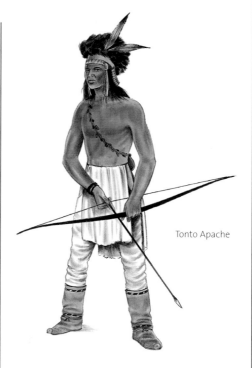

Tonto Apache

Western Apache

fierce warriors, and all of them, with the exception of the Kiowa Apache, were remarkable basket weavers.
- The Apache came from the north in the tenth century (certain authors have advanced the theory of a much earlier migration). From the seventeenth century on, they carried out an ongoing battle with the Spanish and the Comanche, while looting from the peaceful Pueblo peoples. After the annexation of New Mexico, a treaty between the Americans and the Apache was signed in 1852, but the hostilities returned quickly, under the direction of chiefs such as MANGUS COLORADO and COCHISE. Cochise signed a treaty in 1872. After a short-lived truce, the Apache once again entered into

23

Western Apache

conflict (1876–1886) with Victorio and GERONIMO as their chiefs.
• There are Apache reservations in New Mexico, Arizona and Oklahoma. Estimated at a population of 5,000 in 1680, there may be nearly 50,000 Apache today.

Apalachee
• From the Choctaw word *Apalachi*, meaning "People of the other side" (of the Alabama River).
• Language: Muskogean.
• Settled in northwest Florida.
• May have come from west of the Mississippi in about the fourteenth century, bringing with them the tradition of temples built on mounds. They were formidable warriors, and also fished, hunted, and farmed. The Apalachee traded with the Timucua.
• Converted to Christianity by Spanish missionaries in the seventeenth century, the Apalachees were victims of the CREEK and the English colonists (1703). The survivors supported the revolt of the Yamassee (1715).

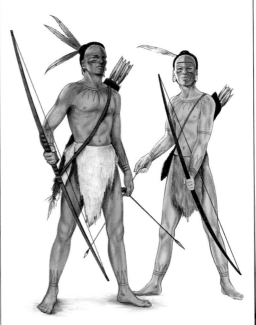

• At the beginning of the nineteenth century, the Apalachee nation no longer existed.

Appaloosa
A name derived from *Paloos*, the name of the tribe living on the banks of the Palouse River in the states of Washington and Idaho. The Appaloosa is a breed of

nomadic lifestyle of BISON hunters. Like all the Plains tribes, the Arapaho moved their camps according to the bison migration.

• Together with the Cheyenne, they fought against the Dakota, the Kiowa, and the Comanche until the peace treaty of 1840. They were then at war against the Shoshone, the Ute, and the Pawnee. The Arapaho joined the Cheyenne and the Sioux in fights against the whites until the Medicine Lodge treaty (1867) and their exile to OKLAHOMA.

• There were 3,000 Arapaho at the end of the eighteenth century. Today, there are an unknown number, maybe 4,000 to 5,000 on two reservations, one in Wind River, Wyoming, and the other in Oklahoma with the Cheyenne.

horse developed by the Indians of the Northwest United States, and they are remarkable for their coat, which is light-colored with brown markings (*see also* Horse).

Arapaho

• From the Pawnee word *Tirapihu* or *Carapihu*, meaning "traders." The Arapaho called themselves *Invna-ina*, meaning "our people." To their allies, the CHEYENNE, the Arapaho were the *Hitanwo'iv*, meaning "sky people."

• Language: Algonquian.

• The Arapaho were sedentary at first. After coming from Manitoba, they crossed Missouri and migrated to the south and to Wyoming, where they adopted the

25

Arikara

• From the Pawnee word *Ariki*, "horn," in reference to their hairstyle. They called themselves *Tanish* or *Sannish*, meaning "the people." In sign language, they were called the "corn eaters."
• Language: Caddoan.
• Settled on the banks of the MISSOURI, between the Cheyenne River and the mouth of the Platte (North Dakota), near the Mandan and the Hidatsa.
• Although they spoke a different language, the Arikara's way of life was similar to that of the Mandan and the Hidatsa: beautiful deerskin clothes, huts made of earth, villages surrounded by barriers, and cultivation of corn.

• At the end of the eighteenth century, they had good business relationships with the French. They were visited by LEWIS and CLARK in 1804. Drawn into conflicts between fur traders, they were also on the route that emigrants took toward the West. The Dakota and smallpox (1837 and 1856) annihilated them. In 1880, the Arikara, the Mandan, and the Hidatsa were put together on the Fort Berthold reservation in North Dakota.
• There were 3,000 Arikara in 1780, and 460 in 1970.

Art

Indians expressed their artistic sense and skill in numerous ways. It is possible to divide their creations into two categories.
• Objects related to functional and daily use: clothing, pottery, weaving, basket weaving, jewelry, knick knacks, and the like.
• Objects and methods of expression that accompanied religious ceremonies or rituals: sculptures, masks, musical instruments, music, dance, and so on.

Because of their richness and variety, we have given each of these topics its own entry (*see* jewelry, dance masks, music, pottery, weaving, basket weaving, clothing, etc.).

Assiniboine

• From the Ojibwa *Usin-upwawa*, "he cooks with stones." The Dakotas called

• The Assiniboine came from the Yanktonai in the seventeenth century and kept their distance from other Sioux tribes, allying themselves with the Cree against the Dakota. They also waged an incessant battle against the SIKSIKA. They were hard-hit by smallpox in 1836.

• There were 8,000 Assiniboine in 1829; 4,000 after the smallpox epidemic; and 2,800 in 1985 in RESERVATIONS in Montana and Alberta.

Athabascan

See Languages, pg. 14.

Atsina

• From *Atsena*, a Blackfoot term meaning "gut people." They called themselves *Haaninn* or *Aaninena*, "white clay people." This tribe came from the Arapaho, who called them *Hitunewa*, meaning "beggars." To the French, they were the *Gros-Ventres*, "big bellies" (of the Plains), which resulted in a frequent confusion with the Hidatsa, known as the *Gros-Ventres* of the River.

• Language: Algonquian.

• After coming from Manitoba, the Atsina occupied northern Montana, along the Missouri River.

• They were nomadic hunters.

• Along with the Blackfeet, they vehemently opposed trappers and were indomitable adversaries of the Sioux (Crow, Dakota, Assiniboine) until 1867,

them *Hohe*, "rebels," and the French, the *Guerriers de pierre*, meaning "stone warriors."

• Language: Siouan.

• The Assiniboine came from the east and from lakes Winnipeg and Nipigon. At the end of the eighteenth century, they were settled in southern Canada, along the Saskatchewan and Assiniboine rivers.

• They had the reputation of being welcoming; they were nomadic and hunted BISON.

Attakullakulla
(1700-1780)

• Attakullakulla was a Cherokee chief, known to the whites as *Little Carpenter*. In 1730, he was part of a delegation of Indian chiefs to England, and decided to gamble on an alliance with the British in order to safeguard his people's independence. Despite his skill and diplomacy, the successive treaties signed with England required the CHEROKEE to cede large parts of their territory.

when they allied themselves with the Crow against their protectors, the Blackfeet, and were severely defeated.
• There were 3,000 Atsina in 1780. In our times, there are about 1,000, on a RESERVATION in Fort Belknap, Montana, which they share with the Assiniboine.

B

Badlands

In this desolate, mountainous region, crossed by deep canyons in western North Dakota, there was a battle that lasted several days in August 1864 between the Sioux and a group of pioneers protected by General Alfred Sully's forces.

Bannock

- *Bannock* is a contraction of the group's proper name, *Bana'kwut*.
- Language: Shoshone.
- First inhabited southeastern Idaho, then western Wyoming and southern Montana.
- Owning horses since the beginning of the eighteenth century, the Bannocks hunted BISON. They moved around in small groups, living in reed huts covered with braided grasses in summer and in small shelters that were partially underground in winter. They fished for SALMON and were skilled basket weavers.
- Proud and sensitive, the Bannock suffered from smallpox EPIDEMICS. They had ongoing conflicts with the Blackfeet, Nez Perce, and, later, the whites. Defeated by the U.S. Army at Bear River in 1863, they were sent to the Fort Hall Indian Reservation in Idaho. Unsuccessful uprising in 1878.
- The Bannock tribe, with a population of around 5,000 in 1829, was estimated to have 1,000 members in 1990.

Basket weaving

Basket weaving was the specialty of the tribes of the southwest (Hopi, Papago) and especially those of the Pacific

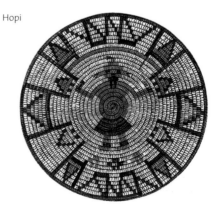

Hopi

29

Pomo

Tlingit

canus) was nevertheless hunted for its fur, which adorned chiefs and shamans. Bear fat was used to make mosquito repellent paste, and bear claws were decorations endowed with mysterious powers. *See also* Grizzly.

Beaver

• As they were called by the English, in reference to their true name, *Tasttine*, which meant "those who live with the beavers."
• Language: Athabascan.
• Occupied the upper regions of the Peace River, at the western edge of the present-day Canadian province of Alberta.

coast, from south to north (Chumash, Washo, Karok, Tlingit). But it was in the POMO tribe that the most elaborate work was carried out, and this continues in our times!

Bear

The object of great veneration by the Indians, the black bear (*Ursus ameri-*

Beaver

Common throughout the entire North American continent, the beaver (*castor canadensis*) inhabited the marshes and banks of lakes and waterways. Willow, birch, aspen and maple trees provided the beaver with food and construction materials. Its pelt was important in trade with the Europeans from the seventeenth century on.

Beliefs

The Indians did not have a religion per se, but they had beliefs. They believed that their world was populated by evil powers that were to be feared, or beneficial powers that were to be honored. To the Indians, this aura of forces must have been in the image of the natural environment surrounding them: infinite, powerful, mysterious, majestic, charged with danger, but also prodigious in its kindness. Thunder, lightning, tornadoes, and other calamities were evidence of the moods of these forces; cold, blizzards, and droughts were a price to be paid for nature's gifts: light during the day, the renewal of spring, abundant game, fresh water in lakes and streams, flowers, fruits, birds and their very decorative feathers.

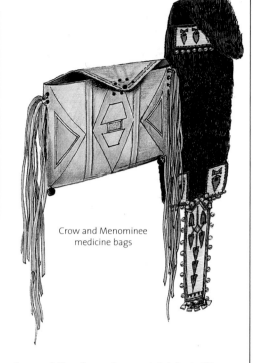

Crow and Menominee medicine bags

For Indians, everything that exists, whether living or not, has a spirituality: people, animals, plants, stones, the earth, so many elements all interrelated by mysterious ties between them. There were many BISON on the plains, not because of an unchangeable cycle but because an Indian prayed to the SPIRITS with conviction, and they answered the person's prayers. These spirits had to be passionately evoked so that nothing disturbed the correct order of things, so that the sun would rise each morning, so that spring would follow winter, so that the hunt would be successful or the harvest would be plentiful.

When an Indian was still a teenager, he had to leave his family for many days while observing a strict fast. The first animal that he dreamed of became his protector, and supplied the skin for his "medicine bag." Once this was done, the Indian was never to kill an animal of that kind, or else he himself would be destroyed. This "medicine" was a set of objects and talismans that each warrior carried on his body and that no one was allowed to see. He could not do without it, not to take care of himself but to protect himself and find omens to guide his decisions.

The warrior had a second, less secret medicine bag in which he kept his CALUMET, his tobacco, his paintings, and some personal talismans that were keepsakes from hunting or from war exploits.

31

Bella Bella

- Origin of this name is unknown.
- Related to the Wakashan group and the Kwakiutls.
- Found on the coast of British Columbia, near the Queen Charlotte Islands.
- In contact with Europeans since 1775, they were then visited by American and English explorers and traders.
- Population of 2,700 in 1780 and 850 in 1906.

Sun Masks (Bella Coola)

Bella Coola

- Corruption of their proper name, *Bilxula*.
- Language: Salishan.
- Basin of what is today the Bella Coola River in British Columbia, north of Vancouver.

- Their economy was based on FISHING and salmon.
- Visited between 1793 and 1894 by European explorers, Methodist missionaries, gold seekers, Hudson Bay trappers, Norwegian settlers, and American lumberjacks. This tribe was decimated by disease and alcoholism.
- The few remaining descendants are on a reservation in British Columbia.

Beothuk

- "Man" in their language.
- Their language is now extinct.

- Inhabited the island of Newfoundland.
- The Beothuk would have had contact with the VIKINGS around the year 1000, with John Cabot's expedition in 1497, and then with European explorers and fishermen, particularly the French. Progressively pushed to the northern part of the island, the Beothuks disappeared sometime during the nineteenth century.
- Population estimated at 500 people in the year 1600.

Berdache

A term on loan from the original French (which has a pejorative connotation) used to designate the *Hee-man-eh*, or young boy who at puberty preferred the women's way of life and would forsake masculine ways. He was not to be a hunter or a warrior, but rather, clothed in a dress, took pleasure in the activities normally assigned to women. Far from being looked down upon, the berdache was, on the contrary, listened to and respected—a mysterious and unusual personality.

Big Foot
(circa 1850-1890)

Sioux chief, who along with 350 Hunkpapa members, was surrounded by the U.S. Army at Wounded Knee, while trying to get to the Pine Ridge Reservation. He died there, along with the other members of his tribe, on December 29,

1890, killed by Army machine gun fire. Along with the murder of Sitting Bull, this massacre marked the end of the Plains Indians' resistance.

Bison

The region where there were bison included, to the north, the southern parts of what are today the Canadian provinces of Alberta, Saskatchewan, Manitoba, the entire Great Plains in the middle of the United States, and, to the south, a large part of Texas—covering an area that is eight times greater than that of France. Always in search of new pastures, the huge herd of bison (60 million head at the beginning of the nineteenth century) each year followed an uninterrupted migration within this vast expanse of territory. In spring the great herd would ascend toward the northwest, and in fall it returned to the southeast. At certain times, as if pushed forward after being spooked, the animals would stampede and it was like a river of hundreds of thousands of animals that moved forward for days upon days. The males weighed more than a ton and the females weighed between 1,400 and 1,700 pounds (650 to 800 kilograms). During their migration, the herds were accompanied by packs of WOLVES or COYOTES, predators who were always ready to take down old or ailing bison. For the Indians, the HUNT for bison was "open" all year round, but two seasons were the most important: in spring, to replenish dwindling reserves and acquire fresh meat, and, at the end of summer, to complete restocking of food as the winter season approached.

In addition to the meat of the bison which was eaten fresh, dried, or powdered (PEMMICAN), the Indians used all parts of the animal's carcass.

• The hide: thickest part (withers) used to create SHIELDS; the softest leathers used to make clothes, MOCCASINS, or covers. The other parts, pieced together, will be used to make tipis.

• The bones: depending on their size and shape, after being sculpted, will be used as shovels (scapulas), TOMAHAWK handles or canoe roll bars (ribs), containers (skulls), and various tools (scrapers, awls, etc.). The largest bones are broken and the marrow is collected for making pemmican, and the small pieces that break off will be used as arrow tips.

• The horns: used to adorn the hair of the most important shamans and warriors. Horns also used as containers for herbs, or, when the Indians use firearms, for powder. No part of the animal will be forgotten, each piece corresponding to a need: teeth (small tools), brain (hide softener), hooves (boiled, they are used in a glue mixture to strengthen shields), bladder (pemmican container), intestines (bow string), tail (fly swatter), and more. Even the bison's manure will be used as fuel.

Bitterroot

The bitterroot (*Lewisia rediviva*) is a small plant with light purple or white flowers and is found where conifers prosper. The roots are edible, and the Indians in the arid regions of the Southwest took advantage of them as a supplementary food.

Black Hawk

(1767-1838)

This chief of the Sauk fought on the side of the British during the Revolutionary War. The Treaty of 1804 required him to relinquish all territory east of the Mississippi. Rejecting the agreement, Black Hawk led his people into a desperate battle. After a long struggle, he finally admitted defeat.

Black Hills

The area located between what is today western South Dakota and northwestern Wyoming. These are "sacred mountains" for the Sioux, the inviolate home of the GREAT SPIRIT, the true center of the universe. In 1874, a military expedition discovered gold there, causing a rush of prospectors even though the Treaty of 1868 clearly prohibited any intrusion into Sioux territory. This was the beginning of a military operation that would finish in 1876 with the Battle of the Little Bighorn.

Blackfeet

• This name comes from the color of their moccasins, which were dyed black—in their language, *Siksika*.
• An Algonquian language.
• Originally from Saskatchewan, they occupied the northern part of Montana and the southern portion of the Canadian province of Alberta, following the Rocky Mountains.
• They were subdivided into three groups from the north to the south: the Siksika, the Kainah (from *Akanina*, which means "many chiefs")—also called Blood Indians due to their face paint, and the Piegan (from Pikuni for "badly dressed robes").
• Very aggressive warriors, the Blackfeet were a dominant people, organized into numerous religious or warrior societies (such as the Ikunuhkatsi, "comrade-in-arms" society). Divided into small nomadic groups

35

for hunting, they would reunite at the end of the summer. The Atsina were under their protection.
• In constant conflict with the Kootenai, the Flathead Indians, and their neighbors the Sioux (Crow and Assiniboine), they also proved to be strong adversaries for trappers. Their dominance started to decline with the SMALLPOX epidemic of 1836.
• Population estimated at 15,000 in 1780; around 32,000 today (half of whom live on RESERVATIONS).

Blowgun
• A long pipe (hollow wood) that was used to shoot small projectiles by blowing. It was primarily used by the Indians of the southeast (Cherokee, Chickasaw, Choctaw) to hunt birds. Their blowguns were effective at more than 65 feet (20 meters).

Boats
For the most part, watercraft were used by native peoples to get from place to place or for FISHING in lakes and rivers. The shapes, lengths, and materials used, along with the techniques used to build them, varied by region. Only boats used for hunting whales were created for use on the open seas.
• Round vessels made of a wood frame covered with bison hide (the Mandan).
• Dugouts created from the trunks of CEDARS, accommodating six to twelve men (Nootka, Makah, Haida and others).
• Canoes holding two to four men with a wooden birch bark frame (Algonquin).
• Single-seat canoes made of rush (Paiute).
• Canoes made of planks coated with tar, holding six to eight men (Chumash).
• Single-seat kayaks made of a wooden skeleton (pine, fir, willow, or other) and then covered in seal or sea lion hide (Inuit).
• Kayaks and umiaks were sealed with seal blubber.

Boats

1 - Mandan skiff
2 - Inuit kayak
3 - Algonquin canoe
4 - Pauite canoe
5 - Umiak
6 - Haida canoe

Two Mandans,
by Karl Bodmer, 1834

Bodmer
Karl (1809-1843)

He was studying painting in Zurich, the city where he was born, when, at 24 years of age, he was chosen by Prince Maximilian of Wied-Neuwied, the German naturalist, to accompany him on a trip to the United States. Arriving in Boston on July 4, 1832, they used the Saint Louis River and then the upper Missouri River to cross Nebraska, the Dakotas, Wyoming, and Montana. They visited many forts and villages, notably the MANDAN villages that neighbored Fort Clark, where they stayed the winter of 1833–1834. Affected by scurvy, Karl Bodmer continued to paint and draw. Upon his return to Europe, Bodmer approached the artists of the Barbizon School. His eighty-one paintings are an important primary source of information about the life and customs of the Sioux Indians.

Boone
Daniel (1734-1820)

American pioneer, who, in 1769, along with five traveling companions explored present-day Kentucky. He founded a settlement there called Boonesborough. Displaced by the government, he settled on the banks of the Missouri River. Boone inspired the James Fenimore COOPER characters Leatherstocking, La Longue Carabine, and Hawkeye.

Bow and arrows

As is the case with most primitive peoples, the bow was the Indians' primary weapon. Made of ash, willow, silver birch, oak, walnut, yew, or cedar depending on the region, the bow's height can vary from 5 feet (1.5 meters)

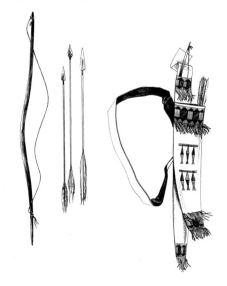

to 6 feet (1.8 meters). The wood is sometimes heat-molded to obtain the ideal curve. The bowstring is most often made from animal tendon but may also be a braid of vegetable fibers or a strip of hide. In rare cases, the bow is made of thin slices of horn formed into a solid piece. This type of bow is shorter, but is a more effective weapon reserved for the most courageous and skilled warriors. The Cheyenne had some bows made of materials that their owners did not recognize; their qualities and their mysterious origin made them extremely appealing.

39

In fact, they were made of whalebone plates, extremely solid blades of up to 6 feet (1.8 meters) in length, which the Cheyenne obtained through trading with the Blackfeet. The use of the HORSE for hunting or war required the Indians to reduce the size of their bows so that horseback riders could handle them more easily. Arrows were arranged in a quiver made of hide (deer, bear, bison, otter, etc.) decorated with colored designs or with feathers and the skins of small rodents. The quiver was placed on the back in a way so that the arrows were easy to grab, and the archer could fire off a shot as fast as possible. The Indians were impressively skilled and quick at this maneuver. According to witnesses, some Indians were capable of shooting eight arrows in less time than it took for the first arrow to fall to the ground. Since precision went along with speed, the Indians were very effective hunters and warriors.

The wood for the arrows, chosen for its solidness, was sometimes fire-hardened. Hunting arrows were different from war arrows: the points of hunting arrows were long and solidly attached to make them easy to pull out of an animal. War arrows were more lightly attached in order to stay in the body of the enemy who was hit. At a medium distance of about 33 to 66 feet (10 to 20 meters), the arrows are dangerous and can travel all the way through the body of a human or an animal.

The Plains Indians equipped their arrows with points made of bone chips.

With the whites came iron, and all types of metal fragments were used by the Indians to make arrow heads. But, from the end of the eighteenth century on, shrewd merchants carried out a very lucrative business by exchanging ready-made metal arrow heads for furs.

Bozeman Trail

Trail crossing the valleys of the Powder, Tone, and Bighorn Rivers, which were the Sioux's best hunting grounds. The trail linked Fort Laramie in Wyoming to the gold mines in Virginia City, Montana, and would prove to be vital in assuring that miners and settlers were able to resupply. It was scouted by John Bozeman, who was killed at the beginning of 1866. To make this route safe, the American army command decided to build three forts (Fort Reno, Fort Kearny, and Fort Smith), construction of which could not be completed due to the relentless attacks by RED CLOUD's Sioux, who were reinforced by the Cheyenne and the Arapaho. At the end of this struggle, which lasted from 1866 to 1868, the Treaty of Fort Rice would be signed, granting the Sioux's use in perpetuity of the land to the north of the Platte River.

Braddock
Edward (1695-1755)

Commander-in-chief of the British forces in 1755, General Braddock had no previous experience with the Indian wars. He was defeated and killed at the Battle of MONONGAHELA while opposing a coalition of Americans, French, and Indians.

Brant
Joseph (1742-1807)

Great MOHAWK leader, Thayendanegea became Joseph Brant when his mother married an Englishman. Converted to Christianity, he translated the Bible into the Mohawk language and first participated in war when he was 13 years old. A colonel in the British army, he fought for tribal unification with the hope of legally preserving part of his ancestral lands. A leader in the Iroquois League, he tried also to prevent the Indians from fighting among themselves. He died of grief after accidentally killing his son.

Bry
Théodore de (1528-1598)

Born in Liège, Belgium, Theodore de Bry created an important series of engravings using the narratives reported by the first explorers. These engravings illustrate the discovery of America and its peoples. His work was continued by his sons, Johannes Theodore and Johannes Israel.

Buffalo Bill

See Cody, William.

Buffalo Dance

A dance that the Indians performed before a hunt so as to appeal to the good graces of the BISON spirit. The survival of all the Plains Indians depended on successful hunts.

41

C

Caddo

• The Caddo were a group of tribes spread over the area of three modern-day border states:
– in Texas, there were the Kadohadacho ("real chiefs"). Caddo is an abbreviation of this.
– in Arkansas, the Hasinais ("our culture"), the Anadarko, and the Eyeich.
– In Louisiana, the Natchitoche and the Adais.
• Language: Caddoan.
• A sedentary agricultural people, they also hunted BISON.
• In 1541, the Caddo clashed with de Soto, who recognized their bravery; then, in 1687, the Caddo encountered the survivors of the La Salle Expedition. [Pierre] Le Moyne d'Iberville brought them under French influence at the

beginning of the eighteenth century. The Caddo then clashed with the Choctaw but then became their allies against the Osage at the end of the eighteenth century. In 1835 they abandoned their lands to the U.S. government and settled in Texas. During the Civil War, they supported the Union and were moved to Kansas. They were finally sent to a RESERVATION in Oklahoma with the Wichitas (1902).
• A population of around 2,000 in the eighteenth century; 967 in 1937.

Caddoan

See Language, p. 14.

Cahokia

The Cahokia Mounds site is near the modern-day city of Saint Louis, Missouri, but is located in Illinois; it is evidence of the Mound Builders' civilization. The largest burial mound is 98 feet (30 meters) high and has a base that is 1,000 feet by 720 feet (305 meters by 220 meters). Construction took place in the year 800 A.D. The tribe that lived near this site was called the Cahokia (*see* Illinois).

Calculations

The Indians used a simple system to evaluate quantity, and they may even have used addition and subtraction. But nothing proves that they were able to multiply or divide, and it is likely that they were not concerned with this type of mathematical operation. The simplest method of counting:
– From 1 to 10, the Indians used their fingers.
– From 10 to 90, they simply placed the index finger of their right hand on each finger of the left hand, starting with the thumb (from 10 to 50) and then started over again (from 60 to 90).
– 100 was indicated by facing the other participant, both hands open and linked together by the thumbs, at the height of the right shoulder.

To assess their wealth in bison hides or horses, the Indians used, depending on their region, variations of the decimal system, and, to teach children to count, perhaps they were familiar with methods similar to that of the Korean Chisenbop.

California Quail

Small, sociable bird commonly found in all regions along the Pacific coast, from Vancouver Island [Canada] to southern California, the California Quail (*Callipepla californica*) is notable for the small black crest that adorns

its head. Its plumage is gray-blue.

Calumet

This word comes from *chalumeau*, the word that French missionaries gave to this object. For the Indians, the calumet had a special role linked to the supposed properties of TOBACCO which they believed heightened intelligence and lucidity. The calumet was solemnly smoked for ceremonies celebrating the arrival of important travelers, to call upon the rain, to decide when to go to war or when to negotiate peace. Inhaling the smoke and then exhaling it toward the sky was thought by the Indians to be a way of communicating with the SPIRITS. Passing it from person to person, the pipe strengthened the connection among participants.

Camas

(Camassia quamash).
Type of lily with beautiful blue-purple flowers, commonly found in the Plains and the Great Basin. Its bulb is edible.

Canada

From the word *Kanada*, meaning "village" in the Iroquois language. Before being used to name the entire country in the Jacques Cartier era, the name "Canada" was only used to refer to the region around Quebec inhabited by tribes that spoke Algonquian languages.

Calusa

• According to Hernando [de Escalante] Fontaneda, who was their prisoner for many years, the name means "fierce people," or it could also be a corruption of "Carlos" (as in Charles V).
• Language: Muskogean.
• Lived in southern Florida.
• Archeological excavations indicate that their ancestors lived in the region around 1,400 B.C. Skilled wood workers, the Calusa were farmers and fisher-men. Using the ocean, they traded with Cuba and, perhaps, with the Yucatan. They practiced human sacrifice.
• Their flotilla of eighty canoes expelled Ponce DE LEON in 1513; how-ever, the Spanish were settled in Florida by the end of the century.
• The population is estimated to have been 3,000 in 1650. A century later, several survivors united with the SEMINOLES, and others fled to Cuba.

Candlefish

A small fish, the candlefish was found in abundance along the northern Pacific coast and was sought after for being very rich in oil. Candlefish were caught with a net in large quantities by the TSIMSHIAN, and were prepared in two different ways:
• once the fish was dried, a wick was threaded through its body, and the fish was used as a candle;
• candlefish were stored in a canoe that was half buried in the sand, and which progressively filled with water. When the fish were very rotten, the mixture was heated for a long time and the oil was skimmed off the surface. When it was purified, this oil was enthusiastically traded with the Haida and the Tlingit.

Caribou

- Language: Athabascan.
- Inhabited the upper Fraser River in British Columbia.
- The Carrier were visited in 1793 by Alexander MACKENZIE and then in 1805 by Simon Fraser; they then came into contact with Catholic missionaries, merchants, miners, and, later, settlers in growing numbers.
- Population estimated at 5,000 in 1780 and at 1,600 in 1909.

Carson
Christopher, aka Kit (1809-1868)

American officer who emigrated to Missouri and spent many years as a trapper and hunter. He acquired extensive knowledge of Indian languages and cultures. Nicknamed "lasso thrower," this famous pioneer served as a scout numerous times in the fight to win the West.

Caribou

American version of the European or Asian deer, the caribou (*Rangifer tarandus*) is a sociable animal that often moves about as part of a great herd made up of thousands of heads. In winter, lichens are their principal source of food; during the milder months, they also eat grasses, reeds, mushrooms, and birch and willow twigs. Indians living in Arctic regions use their hides, which are light and very strong, to make parkas, headgear, boots, and mittens.

Carrier

- Name from the word "to carry." It is derived from the fact that for three years, widows in the tribe had to carry the ashes of their deceased husbands in baskets. Their true name was the *Takulli*: meaning "people who travel by water."

Cartier
Jacques (1491-1557)

French Navigator and explorer, he reached CANADA in 1534 and took possession of the lands he discovered in the name of his king, Francis I of France. A year later, during a second voyage, Cartier visited Algonquin villages via the Saint Lawrence River. After spending the winter near current-day Quebec, he took a dozen Indians back to Saint-Malo, France.

45

Catawba

• Possible origins of the term include the Choctaw *katapa* word meaning "divided or separate," or the Yuchi term *kotaba*, meaning "strong men." Also known as the *issa* or *essa*, meaning "river."

• Language: Siouan.
• Inhabited the Wateree (or Catawba) River Valley in North and South Carolina.
• Sedentary farmers, the Catawba were renowned for both their bravery and their hospitality.
• Confederation consisting of around fifteen tribes. Enemies of the Cherokee, the Catawba aligned themselves first with the British (except for the Yamassee uprising of 1715), and then with the Americans.
• Harshly affected by the wars and smallpox, only a few hundred of them remained in 1775. Some of them mixed with the Cherokees in exile. The last pure-blooded Catawba died in 1962.

Catlin
George (1796-1872)

Born in Pennsylvania, George Catlin received a law degree but decided instead to devote himself to painting. Impressed by the majesty of a delegation of Indians en route to Washington, he undertook an expedition from 1830 to 1836, from the MISSOURI Valley to the southwestern regions, and created 470 pictures of different tribes. Starting in 1837, he showed his works during travels through the United States and Europe (Holland, England, France).

Catlinite

Type of red argillite rock from quarries in Minnesota. The Indians used it to make the bowl of their pipes and calumets. The painter George Catlin identified the source of this raw material.

Cattail

Cattails (*Typha latifolia*) can grow to 8 feet (2.5 meters) tall and live in mountainous terrain. The young plants were eaten as a salad or boiled, and the roots used to make flour by the Indians of the Great Basin.

The Iowa chief White Cloud, by George Catlin, 1844

Cavelier de La Salle
Robert (1640-1687)

French explorer. Leaving from Montreal, he scouted out lakes Ontario, Erie, Huron, and Michigan. He then reached the upper MISSISSIPPI river and followed it to its end. He claimed these vast territories, which cover thirty states of today's United States, and named them Louisiana in honor of France's Louis XIV. During a second journey, La Salle ran aground on the Texas coast, built several forts, founded Fort Saint Louis, and was killed by the Karankawa.

Cayuga
See Iroquois.

Cayuse
• Unknown meaning. Their true name was *Waiiletpu*.
• Language: Waiiletpu, a branch of Shahaptian.
• Inhabited eastern Oregon.
• Mainly BISON hunters.
• Ferociously waged war from 1847 to 1849 (the Cayuse War), then again from 1853 until the Battle of the Grande Ronde in 1856.
• Settled in a RESERVATION with the Umatilla in Oregon. There were 500 of them in 1780 and 370 in 1937.

Cedar
The American species of the cedar family (Alaska yellow cedar, Incense cedar, Western red cedar, and more) are large conifers, found along the Pacific Coast, from Alaska to northern California. This aromatic wood is easy to work with and was an ideal raw material for Indian housing and dugouts in the Pacific Northwest.

Champlain
Samuel de (1567-1635)

French colonist. He convinced Henry IV to establish a colony in Canada, founded Quebec, explored the Lake Huron and Lake Ontario regions (1608), cemented relations with the Algonquin and the Huron and participated in their struggles against the Iroquois. He defended QUEBEC against the English but had to surrender in 1629. Returned to Canada as governor after the Treaty of Saint-Germain-en-Laye (1632) and continued his pursuit of colonization.

Cherokee

• Etymology undetermined. Either a modification of *Tsalagi*, meaning "cave people," a term that they used to refer to themselves, or from the *Tsiloki* Creek, the word *Tsiloki* meaning "People of different speech."
• Language: Iroquois.
• Inhabited the extreme southern part of the Appalachians (Tennessee, North Carolina).
• Farmers and hunters, the Cherokee were organized into seven clans with complex structures. Their approximately sixty villages were grouped around their "capital," Echota.

• Visited by de Soto in 1540, they were involved in all the struggles that bloodied the region. Pushed toward the West by settlers, they participated in the LITTLE TURTLE revolt and also in the Indian victory at Wabash in 1781. They attempted to build a nation using the white man's model. A constitution was adopted, an alphabet was invented, and a weekly newspaper, the *Cherokee Phoenix*, was published. However, the encroachment of settlers and the discovery of gold in their territory in 1826 hastened their exile to OKLAHOMA, which resulted in the death of many

49

on the TRAIL OF TEARS. The Cherokee's loyalties were split during the Civil War, some of them aligning with the North and others with the South.

• The population was estimated at 25,000 in 1650; it grew to 300,000 in 1990. The vast majority are in Oklahoma, but some, an increasing number, are returning to their ancestral homelands in Tennessee and North Carolina.

Cheyenne

• From the Dakota *Sha Hi'yena*, meaning "people of alien speech." The name they called themselves was *Dzitsi'stas*, "our people." To simplify it phonetically, the French called them the *chiens*

(pronounced "sh-ee-en" and meaning "dogs"). Other Indian tribes called them "men with gashes" (the Arapaho) or "cut skin" (Shoshone, Comanche).

• Language: Algonquian.

• Having come from south of the Great Lakes at the end of the eighteenth century, they moved to South Dakota in the BLACK HILLS region.

• Nomadic bison and deer hunters, the Cheyenne were respected for their large height, their intelligence, and their untamed courage.

• They were severely affected in 1849 by cholera. They waged an intense war against the whites from 1860 to 1878, marked by the SAND CREEK Massacre in 1864, when 300 Cheyenne women and children were killed. They were defeated by Custer at Washita in 1868. Allies of the Sioux, the Oglala, the Hunkpapa, and the Santee, the Cheyenne took revenge at LITTLE BIG HORN on June 25, 1876.

• Now on a reservation in Montana and one in Oklahoma with the Arapaho. Population was estimated at 3,000 in 1780; today it is around 11,500.

Chickasaw

• Unknown etymology.
• Language: Muskogean.
• Inhabited the north of present-day Mississippi.
• Legendary warriors. The men hunted, fished, and built their homes. The women were in charge of crop growing.

Chief Joseph
(1840-1904)

Also known as *Hin-mah-too-yah-lat-kekt*, "thunder rolling over the mountains." Chief of the Nez Perce tribe, a wise and intelligent orator, he had to fight to defend the Wallowa Valley. Notable strategist, he lead his people's 995-mile (1,600-kilometer) retreat toward Canada by outsmarting all the attacks mounted by his enemies. Forced to surrender 60 miles (100 kilometers) from his goal, Chief Joseph and his followers would be exiled to the RESERVATION in Colville in Washington State where he died far from his homeland. The nobility with which he conducted himself inspired the respect of all his adversaries.

Chilcotin
- Their real name, *Tsilkotin*, meant "people of young man's river."
- Language: Athabascan.
- Chilcotin River Valley in Canada (British Columbia).
- Alexander Mackenzie traverses their territory in 1793, and Fort Chilcotin is founded in 1829. Area continues to be populated by employees of the Hudson Bay Company, then miners and settlers.
- The population was estimated at 2,500 in 1780 and 450 in 1906.

- Loyal to the English, the Chickasaw played the same role in the south that the Iroquois played in the north. Refusing to tolerate any incursion into their territory, they fought against the Shawnee (1715 to 1745), the Iroquois (1732), the French (1736), the Cherokee (1769), and the Creek (1795). Becoming part of the FIVE CIVILIZED TRIBES, they migrate toward Oklahoma in 1822 where they acquire a clearly defined territory (1855). There were around 20,000 descendants at the end of the twenieth century.

51

Child

Like most societies, Indians considered their descendants to be a treasure for the community. An Indian WOMAN kept her child in a cradle that she could carry on her back or hang from the branch of a tree close to where she was working (*see* Papoose). Indian children were breast-fed until 3 or 4 years of age. As soon as they were able to walk, children moved about in complete freedom, and were progressively initiated into their

responsibilities as future adults. Children were trained by their mothers in the tasks assigned to their sex. Boys were brought up by the men, who introduced them to the techniques of HUNTING and FISHING. In this way, young boys developed their skill and strength to become brave fighters. In addition, they were required to obey the discipline imposed by the older men. So, any young hunter who didn't follow instructions was severely punished. As most tribes followed a matrilineal system of organization, the mother's brother (or another man from the mother's bloodline), and not the father, was responsible for each boy's education. Learning about sexuality happened naturally; sexual relations at a young age were not forbidden, since the Indians did not see this as a fault or a sin. The passage from adolescence to adulthood was always accompanied by an initiation ritual and tests, which were sometimes cruel.

Chinook

• From *Tsinuk*, the name given to them by their neighbors, the Chehalis. They were also nicknamed "Flatheads" because they deliberately reshaped the heads of their children as they grew.
• Language: Chinookan. Should not be confused with Chinook, the trade language used in region in the nineteenth century to promote commerce.
• Occupied northern part of the Columbia's estuary, near the site of Seattle.

• Fishermen, the Chinook also proved themselves to be important in encouraging trade among tribes and then among Indians and whites.
• Englishman John Meares encountered them in 1788 while in search of furs; the LEWIS AND CLARK expedition visited them in 1805. The Chinook were devastated by SMALLPOX in 1829. Their survivors were gradually absorbed by other tribes like the Chehalis.

Chipewyan

• Contraction of the Algonquin-Cree word *chipwayanawok*, meaning "pointed skin," in reference to their Athabascan parkas.
• Language: Athabascan.
• Territory located between Slave Lake in the northwest, Athabasca Lake in the southwest, and the Hudson Bay to the east.
• CARIBOU hunters and fishermen. Father [Emile] Petitot credited them with the same qualities as their neighbors: "innocent and natural in their lifestyle and practices, with good sense and a taste for justice."
• Historical enemies of the Algonquin Cree, the Chipewyan had to concede to

the latter when the whites arrived in 1717 and the fur trade expanded. They were pushed toward the north and the west, up until the time of the SMALLPOX epidemic in 1779 that severely affected both tribes.
• There were 3,500 at the beginning of the eigthteenth century, but 4,643 descendants in the 1970 census.

Chippewa
See Ojibwa.

Chiricahua
See Apache.

Chitimacha

• Uncertain etymology. Perhaps from the Choctaw for "those who have pots" or "those who cook in pots."
• Language: Chitimachan, small linguistic group common with the Washas. Territory on the edge of the Mississippi Delta (current-day Louisiana).
• They were farmers (corn, beans, squash, and other), hunters, and fishermen; the women were expert basket weavers.
• Despite a treaty with Iberville in 1699, the Chitimacha went to war

53

with the French and were reduced to slavery after 1718. Blended with the Acadians.
• They numbered 3,000 in 1650 and around 100 in 1910.

Chiwere
• Term used by the Oto tribe. They called themselves *che-wae-rae*, meaning "those who belong to the earth."
• Designates a group of tribes using Siouan languages—the Oto, the Iowa, and the Missouri tribes, the latter being related to the Winnebago.

Choctaw
• Unknown etymology. May be a corruption of the Spanish word *chato*, meaning "flat" or "to flatten" (the head

of children, because, they thought, this custom resulted in a penetrating gaze). For this reason, the French called them "Flatheads."
• Language: Muskogean.
• Inhabited southern Alabama.
• Less bellicose than their neighbors and enemies the Chickawa, the Choctaw focused on farming (corn, sweet potatoes, sunflowers). They also hunted using BOWS and BLOWGUNS.
• After the de Soto expedition passed through, they had no contact with Europeans for 150 years. Allied with the French, they had to emigrate to the western part of Mississippi in 1780 after the latter were defeated. Members of the FIVE CIVILIZED TRIBES in 1830, they surrendered their land to the U.S. government and moved to OKLAHOMA.
• They numbered around 20,000 in 115 villages at the beginning of the eighteenth century. The 1990 census indicated more than 80,000 descendants in Oklahoma and Mississippi.

Chumash
• Unknown etymology. Also called Santa Barbara and Santa Rosa Indians.
• Language: Hokan.
• Southern coast of California and some of the Santa Barbara Channel Islands.
• Mainly fishermen, the Chumash were accomplished wood and stone workers; the women excelled at BASKET WEAVING.
• Were visited by the Portuguese explorer Cabrillo in 1542. From 1771, five Franciscan MISSIONS were estab-

through the Missouri region and, via the Rocky Mountains, reached the Columbia River, which they followed to its end (May 14, 1804 to September 23, 1806).

Cochise
(circa 1812-1874)

Chiricahua Apache chief. Strong and muscular, he was also loyal and honorable. Confronted by the treachery of the white invaders, he devoted his life to fighting without mercy, organizing raids against isolated ranches, mines, stagecoaches and more. After the Civil War, Chochise refused to lead his people to a reservation in New Mexico, went underground and united the Apache nation with GERONIMO. Captured, he escaped and spent his last days in Arizona.

Cochise People

The evidence of these people's presence was found near Cochise in Arizona. Dating to 10,000 years B.C., these remains bear witness to the primitive culture of these people who had to adapt to climate change (warming after an ice age) and who shifted from gathering to rudimentary farming.

lished in their territory. These new living conditions led to revolt in 1824.
• Estimated at a population of 2,000 around 1770, they have been reduced to several dozen today.

Clan
See Tribe.

Clark
William (1770-1838)

After the Louisiana Purchase, this officer signed on with Meriwether LEWIS to explore new territories with the goal of opening them for settlement. They went

Cody
William (1846-1917)

Cody was better known by his nickname, Buffalo Bill. He began his career

55

as a scout for the U.S. army. His reputation grew as a buffalo hunter and for battling the Indians at the side of General  CUSTER against the Cheyenne and the Sioux (1870–1876). His exploits were popularized by numerous novels, and Buffalo Bill made his fortune by creating a Wild West Show, an extravaganza that he produced in the United States and Europe.

Cœur d'Alène

See Skitswish.

Columbia

- True name: Sinkiuse.
- Language: Salishan.
- Territory was along the upper Columbia River.
- Salmon fishermen.
- Population estimated at 10,000 at the end of the eighteenth century before the smallpox epidemic. It was 52 in 1910.

Comanche

- It is said that their name comes from the Spanish *camino ancho*, meaning "wide trail," or from the Ute term *Kohmahts*, meaning "enemy." They called themselves *Nemene* or *Nimenim*, meaning "the people."

- Language: Shoshone.
- Nomadic bison hunters, they would at times also practice farming.
- They were recognized for their extraordinary horsemanship, their courage, their impulsiveness, their sense of honor, and their conviction that they were superior men.
- Originally from eastern Wyoming (where they were related to the Shoshone). A few migrated toward the south. During the eighteenth century, the Comanche fought against the Spanish

Comanches

Cooper
James Fenimore (1789-1851)

American writer, born in Burlington, New Jersey, and known for his adventure novels, the most famous of which, *The Last of the Mohicans*, remains a classic in this genre. He had firsthand knowledge of Indian cultures, which gave a truthfulness and believability to his narratives.

Cornplanter
(1735 –circa 1840)

Ki-on-twog-ky meaning "corn plant." A Seneca chief who had an Indian mother and an Irish father. Allied with the French against the British in the Battle of Monongahela, he later allied with the British against the Americans. He died a centenarian.

Coronado
Francisco Vasquez de (1510-1554)

Spanish conquistador. In 1540, under orders from the viceroy of Mexico, Antonio de Mendoza, he led a large expedition north. He was to find Cibola, the mythic city "paved in gold," which is said to be located beyond the Rio Grande. Coronado punctuated his travels with atrocities and massacres, going as far north as current-day Kansas in

and the Apache before taking on the Americans. Strong from their alliance with the Kiowa, they increased their pillaging and killing at the beginning of the nineteenth century. After several treaties that were not honored, in the treaties of 1865 and 1867, the Comanche accepted refuge in a reservation in Oklahoma. However, they continued their raids until they were definitively defeated in 1874–1875.
• Population estimated at 7,000 members in 1700 and 11,600 in 1990.

search of the other myth, Quivira, and returned at the end of two years. He did not find gold, but he has much blood on his hands.

Costanoans

• From the Spanish word *Costanos*, meaning "coast-dwellers."
• Language: Penutian.
• Found between what is now the San Francisco Bay and Monterey, 125 miles (200 kilometers) to the south.
• Population estimated at 7,000 in 1770, around 100 in 1910, and extinct in 1930.

Counting Coup

The worth of an Indian warrior was measured by his bravery and his deeds, and specifically the number of *coups*, or strikes, that he was able to carry out against his adversaries. The coup stick was used for this purpose [striking the enemy], but coups could also be carried out bare handed, and in that case, were worth even more since the primary goal was not to kill one's opponent. This custom, common among the Great Plains Indians, showed much about tribal warfare: short, successive skirmishes, such as horse stealing, or, if there were many participants, a battle between two champions. Whatever the situation, it was never about appropriating the land of another, but rather about maintaining freedom of access.

Cowichans

• The meaning of their name is unknown.
• Language: Salishan
• Tribe settled in the southeast part of Vancouver Island.
• They were successively in contact with the Spanish, the English and the Americans; the arrival of the *Hudson Bay Company*, the foundation of the city of Victoria in 1843 and the mining rush surely sealed the disappearance of their way of life.
• There were 5,000 Cowichans in 1780 and 1,300 in 1907.

Coyote

A carnivorous canine, *Canis latrans* is common throughout all of North America. It is known for its sharp, ear-piercing cries, its running speed, and its tricks to track its prey or escape from its predators. The whites accused it (wrongly) of massacring their livestock; the Indians appreciated it even more. In Indian stories, the coyote is always playing tricks on everyone. Capable of taking on any form it wants, the coyote represents a mixture of every good and bad quality: strength and weakness, courage and cowardice, honesty and lies.

Crazy Horse
Tasunka Witko (circa 1845-1877)

Chief and medicine man of the Oglala Sioux. Known for his incomparable courage as well as his charisma and perseverance, he was, in 1866, one of the architects of the defeat of Captain Fetterman; then he defeated General CROOK at ROSEBUD and on June 25, 1876, participated in the rout of General CUSTER at LITTLE BIG HORN. After the destruction of his camp in January 1877, Crazy Horse surrendered to General Crook in May, along with 2,000 of his people. He was imprisoned and summarily

executed on September 7 of the same year during an alleged escape attempt.

Cree

• A shortened form of *Christinaux*, a French form of *Kenistenoag*, one of their names. The Cree called themselves *Iyiniwok*, "people of the first race."

59

The Athabascans of the north called them *Enna*, "enemies."
• A transitional people between the Algonquins and the Athabascans, the Cree were split into two branches: the PLAINS CREES and the FOREST CREE.

Creeks

• So named because they lived near the Ochulgee River, which the Europeans called Ochese Creek. The Creeks called themselves *Muskoke*, from the name of the dominant tribe.
• Language: Muskogean.
• Their vast territory corresponds to the present-day states of Georgia and Alabama.
• Confederation of tribes gathered around the Muskokes, the Creeks were excellent farmers (corn, squash, sunflowers) and occasional hunters and fishermen. Their villages were fortified.
• Alongside the Tamassees during their revolt (1715), they opposed the Cherokees for dominance of the region (1753) and allied themselves with the English against the French and Spanish. This didn't stop the British colonists from invading their lands. After American independence, the Creeks staged the fruitless Red Sticks revolt (1812–1814) and resigned themselves to integrate into the FIVE

CIVILIZED TRIBES. Their forced exile to the distant state of Oklahoma began in 1836.
• There were approximately 20,000 Creeks at the beginning of the eighteenth century. Their descendants are numerous; 43,000 in the 1990 census, and most of them live on reservations in Oklahoma.

Crockett
Davy (1786-1836)

As a young man, he first distinguished himself as a pioneer and BEAR hunter. After having fought against the Creeks (1815), he was named a magistrate and then a colonel in the Tennessee militia. In 1826 Crockett became the state of Tennessee's representative to the Congress of the United States.

He died on March 6, 1836, while defending Fort Alamo against Mexican troops.

Crook
George (1828-1890)

At the end of the Civil War, President Grant assigned this Cavalry General to "pacify" numerous Indian territories. Crook had some successes, and quickly earned a flattering reputation due to his tactical choices and his use of native SCOUTS. On the PLAINS, he recruited many CROWS to confront the men of SITTING BULL and CRAZY HORSE. In Arizona, he received GERONIMO's surrender on March 27, 1886. An indomitable soldier, Crook has remained famous for his straightforwardness, the value of his words, and the respect that he held for his enemies.

Crows

• They called themselves *Absaroke*, "people of the bird." The French called them *Gens du Corbeau*, meaning

Crows

"crow people," from which comes their English name.
- Language: Siouan.
- Settled in Montana along the Yellowstone River and its tributaries—the Bighorn, the Rosebud, and the Powder, and to the south, the Wind River in Wyoming.
- Separated from the Hidatsas around 1776; the Crows were a proud and aggressive people who distrusted the whites and devoted themselves to hunting bison. Because of their elegance, the French nicknamed them *les Brummels du monde indien*, meaning "the Brummels of the Indian world." They had approximately 10,000 horses.
- Visited by LEWIS and CLARK in 1804, the Crows were permanently at war against the Siksikas and the Dakotas. They served as scouts for the American cavalry.
- There were 4,000 Crows in 1780, and nearly 8,500 in 1990 on a reservation along the Bighorn River in Missouri.

Curtis
Edward Sherif (1868-1952)

Edward Sheriff Curtis was an American photographer. From 1897 to 1930, he undertook a long trip that led him to visit the major Indian nations: Apache, Sioux, Cheyenne, Papago, Hopi, Zuni, Pueblo, and more. His project was to photographically preserve the history of the tribes, their lives, their ceremonies, and their adornments. He was also interested in their social organization.

Collected from village to village, 40,000 images testify to Curtis's determination to record for posterity the memory of a world that the "palefaces" destroyed.

Custer
George Amstrong (1839-1876)

George Armstrong Custer was an American soldier. He was a Northern hero in the Civil War, and became a general at the age of 24. When he was awarded the command of the seventh cavalry regiment, he had thirty-six generals. But his expeditions against the Indians were far from unanimously approved by the "Blue coats" and the pioneers. Having succeeded in uniting all the Sioux and Cheyennes against him, Custer was killed along with 200 men at the Battle of LITTLE BIG HORN on June 25, 1876.

Young Kalispel girl, photo by Edward Curtis, 1910

D

Dakota

• Dakota means "allies" in Santee; the Dakota called themselves *Nakota* in Yankton and *Lakota* in Teton. They formed one of the largest peoples of the Sioux nation.

• Language: Siouan.

• Expelled from the area near the sources of the Mississippi by the Cree in the seventeenth century, at the beginning of the nineteenth century the Dakota occupied a vast territory including all of South Dakota

and parts of the current states of North Dakota, Montana, Wyoming, Nebraska, Iowa, Wisconsin, and Minnesota.

• Until the middle of the nineteenth century, they rarely had conflicts with the whites; the Dakota were largely occupied with affirming their supremacy over their neighbors (Ojibwa, Cree, Blackfeet, Crows, Pawnees or Kiowa). In 1851 the borders of Sioux territory were defined by a treaty. But in 1862, the Santee of Minnesota saw themselves stripped of their best lands in exchange for laughably small payments. On the brink of famine, they took advantage of the Civil War to go on the offensive. The uprising claimed 800 civilian and military victims and 800 Indian deaths. The Santee were defeated at Woodlake on September 22, 1862. In 1863 the U.S. army undertook a campaign of punishment, with the battles of Whitestone and Badlands. The SAND CREEK massacre threw the Cheyenne and the Arapaho into the war, in the battles of Platte Bridge and Wolf Creek in 1865. In total disregard for the treaties, the discovery of GOLD in Montana and in Idaho caused the opening of the BOZEMAN TRAIL. Thus began a new wartime period, lasting from 1865 to 1868, during which Red Cloud and Crazy Horse distinguished themselves. The Fort Rice treaty of April 1868 granted rights to the Indians. In 1872 the government decided to build a railroad track between the mountains of the Big Horn River and the Black Hills. The war began again, marked by the battles of Rosebud (1876) and General CUSTER's defeat at Little Big Horn on June 25, 1876. After this disaster, the U.S. army hunted down the Sioux who took refuge in Canada before returning to their reservation in 1881. In 1889 a Paiute named WOVOKA announced the arrival of an Indian Messiah to expel the white invaders. The GHOST DANCE was meant to bring on this event, and so spread

in the Sioux tribes. This final surge ended in the death of SITTING BULL and the WOUNDED KNEE massacre in 1890.

• The Dakota population was estimated at 25,000 in 1780. In 1970 the Dakota Sioux numbered 2,500 in Canada and 52,000 in the United States. They have reservations in Minnesota, Montana, Nebraska and especially in the Dakotas (in Pine Ridge, Rosebud and Standing Rock). There were 103,000 Dakotas as of the 1990 census.

Dall sheep

This species of sheep is present in most of the mountainous regions of the northern hemisphere. The North American variety is known as the Bighorn Sheep, or mountain goat (*Ovis canadensis*). They are gregarious animals, and are excellent climbers and good swimmers. In the summer, the lambs and ewes form herds of about ten animals. In winter, they descend toward lower valleys along with the rams. There, the animals are the most vulnerable to predators such as wolves, coyotes, bears, and lynx. During warmer seasons, the only threat on their steep slopes is from golden eagles.

Dance

As a display of joy or an expression of praise, dance was an important element of all social (gratitude for good harvests), war (departure or return of an expedition, safeguarding the warriors' lives), and religious (thanking the SPIRITS for their kindness during the past year) ceremonies.

SOCIETIES, clans, and tribes had their own specific dances, and dances were also specific to certain circumstances, such as the Scalp Dance, the Calumet Dance, the Hoop Dance, the Snake Dance, and the Sun Dance. Some were reserved for men; some for WOMEN, for example the squaw dance or the dance that was done in the absence of warriors who had left for the hunt, to ensure their success. There were individual dances done by a shaman, and others involved many participants, with their numbers limited only by the available space.

Very specific "steps" showed the theme of the ceremony. For example, in the Buffalo Dance, the dancer's foot might touch the ground and slide rapidly to the back, imitating a bison pawing the ground before charging.

Dekanawida

("Two river currents flowing together")

A fifteenth century prophet, probably of Huron origin, who inspired the founding of the five-nation IROQUOIS confederacy.

Delaware

• From the name of Lord de La Warr, the governor of Virginia. Called themselves the *Lenni-Lenapes*, meaning "real men" or "men among men."
• Language: Algonquian.
• Settled in the states of Delaware, New Jersey, and eastern Pennsylvania.
• Hunters, fishermen, and farmers. Respected by other Algonquin nations because of their supremacy in the region (they were nicknamed "grandfathers.") They were organized into

three clans: *Munsee* (wolf), *Unalachitgo* (turkey), and *Unami* (turtle).

• After getting off to a difficult start with the Dutch, the Delaware chief Tammady signed a treaty with William PENN in 1683, which launched a time of peace that lasted more than 50 years. But Penn's sons despoiled the Delaware of their best lands through the Walking Purchase agreement in 1737. The Indians were then forced into exile in the direction of the Susquehanna and Ohio Valleys.

• The Delaware participated in the final revolts in the east, under the direction of LITTLE TURTLE (1790) and TECUMSEH (1812). During the Civil War, the Delawares fought along side the soldiers from the north.

• There is a Delaware reservation in Oklahoma, with 9,300 Delaware individuals in 1990.

De Soto
Hernando (1499-1542)

De Soto was a Spanish conquistador and accompanied Pizarro to Peru. In 1532 he was convinced that there were fabulous riches to the north. He landed at Tampa Bay on the west coast of Florida in 1531 and, with his approximately

67

DHE

1,000 men, traveled northward and began a bloody voyage, crossing the territories of the Timuca, Cherokee, Creek, Chickasaw, and Mobile. The expedition reached the Mississippi River in 1542, where de Soto died of a fever. After having tried to clear a passage to Texas, the expedition went down the Mississippi on boats that they built from scrap material. They were constantly attacked by Natchez Indians and finally reached Mexico with no more than 300 Spaniards left.

Dhegiha
("on this coast")

This term designates one of the branches of the Siouan group, including the Omaha, Ponca, Osage, Kansa, and Quapaw tribes. In the fifteenth century, they formed, along with the Chiwere and the Winnebagos, a large nation to the north of the Great Lakes. During their migration to the south, they left the Winnebago along the banks of Lake Michigan and separated themselves from the Chiwere. Keeping certain traditions from the great forest, they opted for a semi-nomadic lifestyle, combining agriculture and bison hunting.

Dog

Dogs likely ran alongside the first hunters that crossed the Bering Strait. The first white observers described numerous, noisy dogs in the Indian villages and encampments. Sufficiently domesticated to accompany hunters or to play the role of guard dog, they were not always rewarded for their loyalty since, unfortunately for them, their meat was considered a special food and reserved for honored guests. Dogs were used to tow TRAVOIS; every day, they transported 65 to 90 pounds (30 to 40 kilograms) of gear for 3 to 6 miles (6 to 10 kilometers), but their usefulness was limited. In contrast to other tribes, the Canadian Chipewyan demonstrated a noteworthy attachment to their dogs. They were convinced that men and dogs had common origins. Their dogs were well fed and well treated, and when winter relocations took place, it was not the dogs that pulled the sleds, but the WOMEN!

Dogrib

• Their name, *Thlingchadinne*, meant "dog flank people." According to a legend, this tribe came from the union of a woman and a supernatural being who was half man, half dog.
• Language: Athabascan.
• Their territory separated Great Bear Lake and Great Slave Lake in Canada's Northwest Territory.
• They lived in harmony with their neighbors the Slaves and shared their reputation as a peaceful people. The Dogrib were tall and did not communicate very much. They hunted CARIBOU and musk oxen. They wore mustaches and beards.

• The Dogrib were pushed northward by the incursions of the Crees, and voluntarily excluded themselves from trading in furs for fear of crossing into the territory of rival tribes.
• Their population was estimated at 1,250 in 1670, and there were still approximately 1,000 Dogrib in 1906.

Dog Soldier

See Societies.

Duck

Plentiful game bird of which there are a variety of species. Ducks were present throughout the entire North American continent.

Dull Knife

(circa 1845-1883)

Tah-me-la-pash-me, meaning "Dull Knife," was a nickname given by the Sioux following a battle with a powerless weapon. In reality, his name was *Waviev*: "morning star." Dull Knife was the chief of the northern CHEYENNES and an ally of RED CLOUD. He signed the Fort Laramie treaty in 1868, and went back into battle alongside Sitting Bull and Crazy Horse in 1876. After being hunted down, he was taken prisoner and deported to Oklahoma with his tribe. Refusing to see his people die of hunger, Dull Knife encouraged them to leave the reservation and reclaim their ancestral lands. Betrayed and followed by the army, their wanderings ended at the Fort Robinson massacre on January 9, 1879. With a few survivors, Dull Knife was taken to a reservation on the Tongue River with the Little Tongue band. The Cheyenne were once again in the land of the bison!

E

Eagle

The wingspan of the golden eagle (*Aquila chrysaetos*), which inhabits the continent's mountainous regions, can reach almost 8 feet (2.4 meters). The golden eagle is a powerful raptor with keen eyesight, feeding on rodents and sometimes on larger prey. Its feathers are dark brown with a golden area on the nape of the neck. Young individuals have white FEATHERS with black markings, which are very sought after by Indians to decorate their hair.

The bald eagle has a yellow head, and a slightly smaller wingspan than the golden eagle. The bald eagle is a fish-eater, which lives on the edges of lakes and rivers throughout all of North America except in the Arctic zone. The bald eagle appears on the seal of the United States.

Epidemics

Living on a continent that had long been isolated from the rest of the world, the Indians hadn't developed any natural defenses against illnesses that were common in Europe. From the seventeenth century on, the Indians were contaminated: Whatever the illness and the degree of severity (from the most benign such as scarlet fever and mumps to the most dangerous such as SMALLPOX and cholera), the outcome was always deadly. The first serious epidemics hit Texas, Louisiana, and the areas along the Missouri, Saskatchewan and Columbia Rivers. In the eighteenth century, some epidemics were caused on purpose, for example during the criminal acts of General AMHERST. Then, smallpox hit many tribes of the Great Plains from 1815 to 1837: the Assiniboine, Arikara, Comanche, Pawnee, and Blackfeet. When the epidemic reached the MANDAN tribe, it disappeared completely (1,569 deaths out of a population of approximately 1,600). From 1854 to 1870, new waves of the sickness reduced the population of the

Crow, Arikara, Atsina, Kiowa, Cheyenne and Cree tribes by 25 to 50 percent. It is estimated that from the sixteenth to the nineteenth century, more Indians died of illnesses than died in wars.

Erie

• The Iroquois called them *Ga-Qua-Ga-O-No*, the Hurons called them *Yenresh*, and the Tuscaroras called them the *Ken-raks*, which the Europeans deformed into "Erie." All of these names referred to the bobcat, a type of lynx, from which came the English name "Cat Nation."
• Language: Iroquoian.
• Their territory was located between the south end of Lake Erie and the upper reaches of the Ohio River. The Erie had villages with a small amount of agriculture (corn), and they also fished.
• Weakened by epidemics and without firearms, the Erie were almost completely eliminated by the Iroquois in 1657. The survivors integrated with their conquerors as captives, and their descendants progressively assimilated into this group.

Eskimo

A pejorative term for the INUITS, used in particular by the Naskapi and the Cree. *Eskimo* comes from the Algonquian language word *Askimon*, meaning "he eats raw," an allusion to the Inuits' custom of eating seal meat without cooking it.

Eskimo-Aleut

See Languages, pg. 12.

Everglades

A vast swampy area in southern Florida, to the south of Lake Okeechobee. Inhabited by abundant game, in particular, alligators, this type of ecosystem is common along the coasts of Florida and in the lower basin of the Mississippi River.

A view of the Everglades

F

False Face Society

For the Iroquois, curing illnesses affecting the head, shoulders, and limbs was the task of the members of the False Face Society. Once they were called upon, the members of this group arrived at the sick person's house and made a circle around the person while wearing fanciful masks. Some of them danced while shaking rattles; others gathered ashes and threw them on the patient. Once the patient was cured, he became a member of the SOCIETY. The masks were very different and very impressive, evoking the original False Face, a supernatural being who was punished by the Great SPIRIT for his boastfulness and condemned to take care of the sick from then on.

Family

Indian marriage did not have the same meaning as in European societies. Even though we can't exclude the possibility that Indian men and women were in love, marriage was more of a contract between two individuals. One of them provided subsistence and safety; the other kept the home and bore children. The future bride's hand was obtained through gifts that the warrior who wanted to marry her gave to his future father in law: food, animal skins, tobacco, horses, and such. The transaction was made only with the future bride's consent. If it was determined that the suitor had proven sufficient generosity, nothing stood in the way of the ceremony: celebrations for the whole village with banquets, dances, and chants celebrating the accomplishments of the brave's family. The union could be broken with the same ease, and without drama . . . but adultery was severely punished. In theory, Indians are monogamous, but nothing stopped a man from having two wives. Far from being a cause for disapproval, this type of situation would bring honor to the courageous husband, since in order to have a large family with many children, it was best to be a talented hunter who could feed his family by bringing back abundant game. For these cham-

pions, the best solution was to marry two sisters: then it was certain that there would be harmony within the family.

Children were very much loved by their parents; nevertheless, they were raised strictly, not out of severity but to toughen them and prepare them to fulfill their roles as adults.

Old women and the few old men enjoyed obvious respect: a long life resulted in vast experience, and their wise opinions were very much listened to. When their declining strength didn't allow them to fulfill their tasks any

more, or even to follow the tribe, they were abandoned, often upon their own request. Then, they peacefully waited to rejoin the land of the Great SPIRIT and its vast hunting grounds.

Feast of the Dead

What scared the Huron about death was the separation of a dead person from his community. The Feast of the Dead was meant to reintegrate the remains of the dead in one place. Dead bodies were dug up, the bones cleaned, and all of them reburied in a common grave. This lugubrious ritual was accompanied by dances and drinking.

Feathers

During wartime or cultural activities, feathers were largely used by the Indians as decorative elements for HAIR STYLES, clothing, calumets, weapons, and the like. The most sought-after feathers were: migrating geese and ducks, eagles, falcons, wild turkeys, crows, woodpeckers, quail, jays, blackbirds, and even parakeets!

In order to compensate for the highs and lows of hunting seasons, the Pueblos and the Indians of Virginia kept captive EAGLES and TURKEYS. In the Northeast, the Algonquins and the Iroquois made patchwork blankets out of strips of bird skin that still had feathers on them. Other peoples used feathers to decorate their BASKET WEAVING, altars or clothing, and when birds' beautiful tail feathers weren't used to make fans, they were an addition to the clothing worn by braves. In addition to their decorative role, feathers signified the combat prowess of the person who wore them. For this, eagle feathers were the most sought after.

Fernandeno

• The tribe's name comes from one of the two Spanish missions built on their territory.
• Language: Uto-Aztec.
• Settled in the Los Angeles Valley in California.
• Their population was estimated at 2,000 in 1770. Today, the tribe has completely disappeared.

Finger Lakes

A series of deep (up to 689 feet/210 meters), narrow, and parallel lakes located in northern New York state, to the south of Lake Ontario. The main lakes, from east to west, are Oneida, Skaneateles, Owasco, Cayuga, Seneca,

Meaning of feathers: 1. Has been wounded in battle. 2. Dealt five "coups" to opponents. 3. Killed or wounded an opponent. 4. Killed an enemy. 5. Killed and scalped an enemy. 6. Dealt four "coups" to opponents. 7. Slit an enemy's throat. 8. Has been wounded many times.

Keuka, and Canandaigua. All of them form the center of the territory of the five-nation IROQUOIS Confederacy. The Iroquois thought that the lakes were created by a divine being's hand being placed on the land.

Firearms

The Indians used the white people's "fire sticks" only little by little. The conquistadors who set off to explore north of the Gulf of Mexico were equipped with crossbows and arquebuses. Although effective, these weapons had a major disadvantage: They were designed for European wars, so they proved to be poorly suited to the battles that the Spanish had to carry out against the Indians. Reloading them required a series of procedures that took from 50 to 60 seconds, in which time a skilled Indian archer

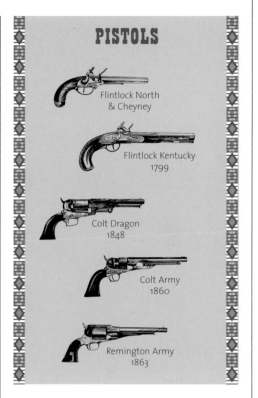

PISTOLS

Flintlock North & Cheyney

Flintlock Kentucky 1799

Colt Dragon 1848

Colt Army 1860

Remington Army 1863

could shoot a dozen arrows at his adversaries. While the Indians were quickly beaten, their arms were not inferior from the point of view strictly of effectiveness. However, the Indians didn't know how to make any improvements to better resist adversaries in small numbers. Was this a question of strategy? Maybe . . . but it was more likely a consequence of the respect that was inspired in the Indians by weapons that worked in mysterious ways, reminding them of thunder and lightning and capable of killing at a distance of many hundreds of yards.

From the beginning of the sixteenth century on, the English, settled around

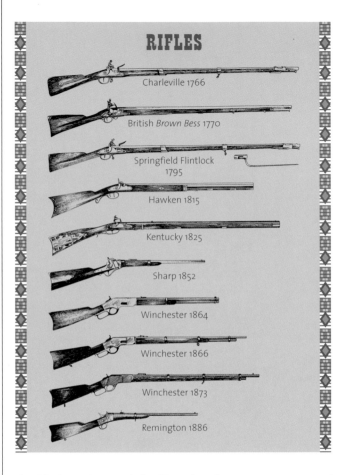

RIFLES

Charleville 1766

British *Brown Bess* 1770

Springfield Flintlock 1795

Hawken 1815

Kentucky 1825

Sharp 1852

Winchester 1864

Winchester 1866

Winchester 1873

Remington 1886

in Upper Missouri. Certain tribes understood perfectly well that once they owned horses and firearms, they were assured of definite supremacy over neighboring tribes. For their part, the Europeans weren't acting innocently when they sold the weapons. The French wanted to get into the Indians' good graces and turn them into allies against the English. The English in turn acted the same toward the French.

Until the beginning of the nineteenth century, the weapons that the Indians owned (muskets or pebble guns) were most often of poor quality, and were either old models or in poor condition. There were very few warriors who deserved to be called good shots; without serious training, they were more inclined to waste their ammunition than to equal the whites in this area. Some Indians were even satisfied to own a gun as a symbol of power, even if the weapon wasn't in a condition to be fired.

Without a doubt, the change from traditional weaponry to firearms was inevitable for the Indians, when confronted with the white world. This also accelerated the process of destruction

the Hudson Bay, and the French, who were active in the Saint Lawrence Valley as far as the Great Lakes, competed to trade with the Indians. The Cree and the Assiniboine, who were their primary contacts, spread European weapons even farther to the west and south. Soon, guns from the east were traded for horses that came from the south, resulting in a twofold distribution of the goods that were the most coveted by the Indians, beginning with the Mandan and Hidatsa villages and death for three reasons: to the detriment of intertribal business relations, the Indians preferred to trade with the whites in order to obtain things that they didn't produce themselves, such as gunpowder, ammunition, and alcohol. This dependency motivated them to intensify their hunt for animals, since furs were their primary exchange currency. In doing this, the Indians disrupted their traditional way of life and participated in the destruction of their environment, a disastrous task that was finished off by the whites in the nineteenth century.

By supplying weapons, the Europeans incited the most aggressive tribes to attack their neighbors. Thus, in the seventeenth century, the Iroquois, who were unwisely armed by the Dutch, successively attacked the Huron, the Neutral, the Algonquin, and the Erie, who were completely exterminated in 1653. Along with these inter-Indian wars came participation in wars between the European powers. Some tribes allied themselves with the French against the English, others allied themselves with the English against the French, while others fought alongside the English against the Americans; Indian tribes were involved in conflicts that were not theirs, and in which they had everything to lose no matter who the winner was.

These effects touched the tribes in the Northeast first, but during the entire nineteenth century, the incessant series of battles carried out to oppose the irresistible invasion of their land by the colonists led the Indians to their defeat by extermination or deportation.

Fishing

All of the Indians who lived along the Atlantic and Pacific fished and gathered crustaceans. Some were notable for their specific methods:
• The Nootka and the Makah of the northern Pacific coast hunted WHALES

from canoes that were from 26 to 39 feet (8 to 12 meters) in length. Their 16-foot (5 meter) harpoon was fitted with points made from seal skin. The enormous mammal was harpooned until it died.
• Farther north, the Eskimos trapped salmon by constructing stone barriers that channeled the salmon toward shallow ponds where they could be easily captured.

The Indians of the interior fished in lakes and rivers, and their techniques varied from north to south:
• Salmon fishing was practiced by the tribes of the northwest. Fish were abundant and the Klikitat and Thompson Indians set up actual traps in rivers, similar to the *bourdingue* traps used in France. The fishermen were also very skilled at harpooning salmon.
The Menominee Indians who lived along Lake Superior and Lake Michigan fished at night and installed lights on their canoes. The fish were attracted to the light and came to the surface, where they were harpooned. This was the Amerindian version of *lamparo* fishing.

• The Cherokee (Tennessee), the Iroquois (New York), and the Chumash (California) practiced a specific type of fishing: they threw powders made from vegetable bark, seeds, or roots into lakes and ponds. The drugged fish came to the surface where it was easy to catch them.

Five Civilized Tribes

Ironic name used to designate the Choctaw, Chickasaw, Seminole, Creek, and Cherokee tribes. At the beginning of the nineteenth century, these peoples had tried to integrate into the young American nation. They converted to Christianity, sent their children to school, and learned farming. They expected, in return, to remain on their lands. But these Indians were obstacles in the way of the expansion of land cultivation, in particular cotton farming. Despite their resistance, they were sent to Oklahoma in 1830.

Flathead

• One of the tribes of the Salish group, most commonly known as Flatheads, an expression that the whites used in reference to the tribes who molded the skulls of young children using a frontal bandage. Misled by the presence of Chinooks (undoubtedly slaves) in the Salish tribes, the Canadian trappers nicknamed this people "Flatheads," even though they never practiced this mutilation.

• The Forest Cree were hunters and fishermen and excelled at paddling their birch bark canoes.
• Strategically located, the Cree were at the heart of French-American competition for the control of fur trading. Allied with their brother people the CHIPPEWA, they had good relations with the whites, to the detriment of the Athabascans of the north and west.
• Estimated at 15,000 individuals in 1776, the Cree population was severely affected by smallpox. After falling to 2,500 in the nineteenth century, today there are approximately 10,000 Cree in Manitoba, and about 5,000 in the Northern Territories.

Fort Laramie

This name comes from a French trapper, La Ramée. The fort was located at the confluence of the North Platte and the Laramie River, in southeastern Wyoming. At first named Fort William, it was the location of the fur company beginning in 1834, and then in 1876, given its strategic position, it became a military fort, equipped with a large garrison.

Four Corners

The point where four American states, Utah, Colorado, Arizona, and New Mexico, meet. This area was occupied by the ANASAZIS 2,000 years ago and has been occupied by the NAVAJOS since the sixteenth century.

• Language: Salishan.
• Lived in western Montana.
• They hunted deer and bison.
• They were inexorably pushed back toward the west by their enemies the Blackfeet. The Flathead lived in peace with the whites and transferred their territory to the government in 1885 in exchange for a reservation in Montana.
• There were 600 Flathead at the beginning of the twenieth century.

Forest Cree

• Occupied the area between the west coast of James Bay and Lake Athabasca.
• Language: Algonquian.

Fox

• Name given by the whites in reference to one of their clans, the Red Fox. Their name, *Meshkwaking*, meant "red earth people."
• Language: Algonquian.
• Settled to the east of Lake Michigan, south of the territory of the Sauk (state of Wisconsin).
• The Fox were semi-nomadic farmers and bison hunters. They had the reputation of being extremely aggressive and were constantly fighting against the OJIBWA.
• In contact with the Europeans from 1660 on, the Fox took the side of the English against the French, who wanted to trade with their enemies the Sioux. Close to extinction, they merged with their neighbors the SAUK, whose endeavors they shared, with the exception of the Black Hawk revolt of 1832.

• There are Fox reservations in Oklahoma (with the Sauk) and in Iowa.

Fox

Two variations of the species share the continent.
• The red fox (*Vulpes vulpes*) is present from the north to the south.
• The gray fox (*Urocyon cinereoargenteus*) is only present in the southern part. Foxes are omnivores and are difficult to see because they prefer to move around at night and hide during the day in small rocky caves, burrows, or hollow trees, preferably oak trees. All of the Indian peoples admired the qualities traditionally ascribed to foxes (trickery, intelligence, etc.) and these animals appear in countless stories and mythological tales of native peoples.

Frémont,
John Charles (1813–1890)

Before entering politics, this son of a French immigrant crossed the unexplored land between the Missouri borders and the southern Rocky Mountains. In 1843 he succeeded in reaching Oregon and the Pacific, coming up against many Indian tribes who blocked his passage. Frémont contributed to the annexation of California by the United States (1850). He was named a general during the Civil War and ended his career as governor of the Arizona Territory.

80

Gabrielino

- Named after San Gabriel, one of the two missions (the other was San Fernando) in the area of present-day Los Angeles.
- Language: Uto-Aztecan.
- Settled along the San Gabriel River, on Santa Catalina island, and along the Pacific coast, as far as present-day San Clemente.
- There were 5,000 Gabrielino (including Fernandino) in 1770. They have disappeared in modern times.

Gall
(1840–1894)

A great strategist and close ally of Sitting Bull, Gall led the Hunkpapa Sioux in the battle of LITTLE BIG HORN on June 25, 1876. After fleeing to Canada, Gall surrendered in January 1881, and in 1889 he accepted the position of tribal judge on the Standing Rock Reservation.

Games

The Indians were game players . . . and devoted gamblers, to the point that it was common for an individual to bet his favorite possessions, sometimes his HORSE or even his wife! While playing dice (made of nut shells, acorns, or small pieces of colored bone), Indians did not hesitate to sing in order to bring good luck or to break their opponents' concentration! But the most valued were skill games and juggling: The Ojibwas and the Iroquois played a game called "the snake in the snow," which involved throwing a long pole as far as possible in a long trench dug in the snow. Another game called on the participants' skill: It involved throwing a spear through a small hoop that was rolled across the ground. The best known game was lacrosse, particularly in the nations in the Southeast. Lacrosse consisted in winning a small leather ball by any means possible. Two teams fought over the ball in a confrontation that could reach rare heights of violence.

Gan Dance

To the Apaches, *Gans* were mountain SPIRITS who had the power to cure illnesses and divert the evil actions of devils. The *Gans* appeared during the Sunrise Dance, a ritual ceremony that

Games

was held when one or more girls reached puberty. The ceremony lasted four days (four was a sacred number), and songs, dances and gift-giving alternated with drinking. Each girl wore makeup and was dressed in yellow, the color symbolizing pollen and fertility. She was assisted by an old woman who told her about the duties and privileges of womanhood. Every night, four dancers symbolizing the *Gans* came out of their mountainous hiding place and joined the ceremony. Their dance happened under the direction of the shaman who had supervised their costumes, the accessories, and the ritual black and white PAINTINGS. The ceremony ended at dawn, at the end of the fourth night. Then, the shaman painted a sun on the palm of his hand and held it above each girl's head.

Geronimo
(1829-1909)

His actual name was Goyathlay, "one who yawns." Geronimo was a chief and medicine man of the Chiricahua APACHE. In 1858 the Mexicans assassinated his wife and his three children; after that, Geronimo spent almost 30 years waging war against the Mexican

and American invaders (colonists, soldiers, and other gold seekers) in New Mexico and Arizona. As the last of the great Apache fighters after the disappearance of COCHISE and MANGUS COLORADO, he tried in vain to oppose the deportation of his people to arid and unhealthy reservations. Geronimo gave in in 1886 and died in Fort Hill, Oklahoma, after dictating his memoirs.

Ghost Dance

A Paiute visionary, WOVOKA, also known by the name "one who makes life," inspired this dance. For the participants, the Ghost Dance prophesied the return of the souls of the BISON and of all the warriors who had died in battle. At the end of the nineteenth century, the Sioux (the Teton Sioux in particular) transformed the Ghost Dance into a ceremony of war and revenge: It predicted that the whites would be annihilated and the Indians would reclaim their territory and their ancestral way of life. The dance was forbidden by the American authorities, who also decided to arrest Sitting Bull, considered to be an instigator of trouble. These tensions culminated in the WOUNDED KNEE massacre on December 29, 1890.

Gold

The search for this precious metal was a strong motivator for the Spanish con-

83

slavery in the mines. The massacre of the Klamath, Hupa, Yurok, Karok, Miwok, and Maidu tribes continued until 1870. In 1874 the discovery of new deposits in the BLACK HILLS, the Sioux's sacred land, attracted new adventurers to another region with equally dramatic consequences.

Goldenrain tree

This is a plant in the sapindaceae family, which grows in the subtropical zones of the United States. Its species, numbering about a dozen, contain saponin. Used as a natural detergent, this foaming substance also acts as a stupefacient on fish, which enjoy eating goldenrain seeds. The Indians also used this technique to fish effortlessly in ponds and lakes.

Goshute

• From *Gossif*, meaning "their chief" and *Ute* (etymology unknown).
• Language: Uto-Aztecan.
• Settled near the Great Salt Lake, in northwestern Utah.
• The group's history is unknown, but they were remarkable in their ability to survive in one of the continent's

quest. Some years later, French navigator and explorer Jacques Cartier thought that he was bringing barrels of gold back from Canada, but this in fact turned out to be only yellow pyrite crystals! But it was a blacksmith named John Marshall who sparked the gold rush in California when he discovered a gold nugget on January 24, 1848, on the land of Captain John Sutter in the southern Sierra Nevada. Hundreds of thousands of prospectors crossed California in every direction in the pursuit of this metal, hunting and killing the Indians or trying to reduce them to most arid regions. When rabbits, birds, and rodents were rare, the Goshute earned their nickname, Diggers, also given to the Paiute, by digging in the dirt to find insects and caterpillars to eat. Snakes and lizards completed their diet.

• The Goshute were not American citizens, so young Goshute refused to go to fight in the war in Europe in 1918 despite attempts at a draft.

• At their height, there were between 10,000 and 20,000 Goshute, and there are about 500 today.

Grant,
Ulysses Simpson
(1822-1885)

A general and statesman, most noted for accepting the surrender of Confederate General Robert E. Lee during the American Civil War, Grant was elected president of the United States in 1868 and was reelected in 1872. Concerned with ending the Indian wars, Grant began his presidency with a policy of reconciliation, which did not achieve all of the results that were hoped for.

Great Serpent Mound

A vestige of the ADENA civilization, located near Cincinnati, Ohio. This is a snake-shaped dirt mound measuring 5 feet (1.5 meters) high and 1,312 feet (400 meters) long. Other Adena sites depict birds, turtles, and human silhouettes.

Green Corn Ceremony

This traditional ceremony of the farming tribes in the southeast (Creeks, Cherokees, Chickasaws, Choctaws) marked the last corn harvest at the end of the summer. It gave thanks for the year's harvest, and expressed hopes that the next harvest would be just as abundant. The ceremony took many days and involved the purification of kitchen utensils, the interiors of houses, and others. It ended with a bath for all of the participants.

Grizzly

Inhabiting the Rocky Mountains from Alaska to Wyoming, the grizzly bear (*Ursus horribilis*) can stand more than 6.5 feet (2 meters) tall when it stands up on its hind feet. This omnivore feasts on diverse types of plants, fruits, mushrooms, insects, small and large mammals, and even carrion. Grizzlies love fish and are adept at catching salmon. The grizzly normally avoids humans; nevertheless they are dangerous due not only to their long sharp claws and teeth but to their unpredictability. The grizzly's thick fur was coveted by the Indians. For the majority of Indians, the bear is a very respected animal and a symbol of strength and wisdom.

85

Certain tribes even call grizzlies "grandfather."

Gros-Ventre

This term leads to confusion. To the French, it designated the Atsina, or the plains Gros-Ventre, resulting in confusion with the Hidatsa, who were also called the river Gros-Ventre.
• Language: Algonquian.
• The plains Gros-Ventre called themselves *A'ainin*, "white clay people."
• The Gros-Ventre hunted bison, and their nomadic tribes were allied with the Blackfeet.
• There are approximately 3,000 Gros-Ventre today, of which half live on the Fort Belknap reservation in Montana, together with the Assiniboine.

Grouse

Similar to the European varieties, the spruce grouse (*Dendragapus canadiensis*) inhabited the subarctic taiga and tundra. Another type of this beautiful bird, the ruffed grouse (*Bonasa umbellus*) shared the same habitat.

Haida

- Their name comes from *Xa'ida*, meaning "people."
- A linguistic isolate.
- Settled on Prince of Wales Island and Queen Charlotte Island, north of Vancouver.
- The Haida were deep-sea fishermen (tuna, cod, halibut, and all types of marine mammals), they dug their large ocean canoes out of red cedar trunks.
- They were remarkable woodcarvers, skilled traders, and renowned warriors.
- The Haida were successively visited by the ships of Juan Perez (1774), Bodega, and La Perouse (1786). They were hardhit by SMALLPOX with 80 percent of their population killed by the illness.
- There were approximately 8,000 Haida in 1760, and 600 in 1915, but they numbered 1,500 in 1968, and today almost 4,000 Haida live on Queen Charlotte Island in Haida National Park.

Hamatsa Society

For the KWAKIUTL, who lived on the southern end of the west coast, the Hamatsa society demonstrated the power of shamans, who recruited men and women who wanted to establish their social position in the tribe. The Hamatsa SOCIETY worshiped the fearsome "Cannibal Spirit," and its initiation ceremonies were terrifying, aiming to reinforce the power of the society's members on the rest of the tribe. During these ceremonies, the shamans wore costumes made of cedar

87

Garces. The Havasupai were farmers and hunters and lived peacefully in their lush paradise, and they are still there!

Headdress

The magnificence of Indian head-dresses epitomizes the legend of its wearer. They differed between tribes and the most elaborate ones were the privilege of important individuals, SACHEM, shamans, or warriors, due to their status or their deeds.

Hiawatha

According to their mythology, there was a time when the Iroquois tribes lived in a state of constant conflict, perpetually involved in skirmishes and the settling of personal disputes. At the beginning of the fifteenth century, a wise man named Dekanawidah ("two river currents flowing together") had a dream: the great IROQUOIS tribes had to stop fighting in order to join together in the confederacy. Hiawatha, a Mohawk warrior, took the message from tribe to tribe, and rallied the five largest Iroquois nations: Seneca, Cayuga, Onondaga, Oneida, and Mohawk. Thus was born the Iroquois Confederacy, also known as the League of Five Nations. The council of the confederacy met every year on the Onondaga's land, at the foot of the Tree of the Great Peace. On the highest branch sat an eagle!

bark, and masks that were painted to look like birds, the friends of the Cannibal Spirit.

Havasupai

• Their name means "people of the blue water"
• Language: Yuman, related to the Hokan language family.
• Settled near Cataract Canyon on the Colorado River (northwest Arizona).
• Living on the margins of history and well-hidden in their canyon, the Havasupai were only discovered in 1776, by the Franciscan Francesco

Indian Headdresses

1 - Blackfoot
2 - Cheyenne
3 - Mandan
4 - Ponca
5 - Sioux Oglala

of life. They did not practice *Okeepa*, but rather the Sun Dance, which also included bodily torture. They had many societies, the "Dog Soldier" for men, the "Society of the White Bison" for women. They received the same visitors as the Mandan and were also afflicted by the SMALLPOX epidemic.

• There were 2,500 Hidatsa in 1830, and by about 1950, approximately 1,000 Hidatsa lived in Fort Berthold, North Dakota. There, they formed a joint tribal government with the Mandan and the Arikara.

Hogan

Hogans are the traditional NAVAJO dwelling. They are circular, made of three poles joined at the center and oriented to three of the cardinal points. Two other posts marked the entrance, which opened to the East. This structure was then covered with wood, bark, and earth.

Hidatsa

• Their name means "willows," the name of one of their villages. The Mandan called them *Minitaris*, "those who crossed the water," in reference to their first meeting on the banks of the Missouri River. The French trappers called them the Gros-Ventre of the River (resulting in possible confusion with the Atsina).

• Language: Siouan.

• Strongly connected to the Crows, the tribe from which the Hidatsa came. Neighbors of the Mandan on the Missouri, they observed the same way

Hohokam

The Hohokam people settled in the Gila Valley in southwest Arizona in 100 B.C. They were skilled at making the best of their water resources and made complex irrigation systems. The ditches that carried the water were deep and lined with clay, which limited evaporation and water loss due to evaporation. Small dams made it possible to regulate the flow rate. In this way, the Hohokam were assured of two annual harvests: one in the spring after the snow melted, and the second at the end of summer. This is why they were nicknamed "the desert farmers." The Hohokam were peaceful. They were also skilled artisans; they made pottery, shell carvings, rock sculptures and weavings. They undoubtedly fell victim to a series of droughts and abandoned their villages in the fifteenth century. The Pima and the Papago are probably their descendents.

Hokan
See Languages, pg. 15.

Holata Micco
(circa 1810-1864)
This Seminole chief, nicknamed Billy Bowlegs, was one of the signers of the Treaty of Payne's Landing on May 9, 1832, by which the SEMINOLE agreed to migrate to Indian territory. But it wasn't until 25 years later, after conflicts that lasted from

1855 to 1858 (the "Third Seminole War") that Billy Bowlegs and his people decided to head for Oklahoma.

Hopewell
A people whose origins are unknown, the Hopewell occupied a vast territory from the Great Lakes to the north to the mouth of the Mississippi to the south, from 100 B.C. to A.D. 350. The Hopewell were skilled potters, and they sculpted wood and worked with copper, stone, and shells. They cultivated corn and built imposing dirt mounds where they buried their dead, surrounded by jewels. The Hopewell formed a prosperous and organized society and traded with other regions to the north and west.

91

(KACHINA worship, the Snake Dance, etc.). Their handicrafts and artistry were particularly remarkable.

• The Hopi society was matrilineal: succession and social status were associated with the mother. WOMEN owned the fields, but only the men could work there.

• The Hopi stood in solidarity with the other Pueblo people against the Spanish invaders, and were also in constant battle with the NAVAJO. Despite the Spanish influence, the Hopi remained resistant to Catholicism and maintained their ancestral culture.

• There were an estimated 2,800 Hopi in 1680. There are probably more than 9,000 today on the Hopi reservation in Black Mesa, Arizona.

Hopi

• Their name is a contraction of *Hopitu*, "those who are peaceful."

• Language: Shoshonean, from the Uto-Aztecan family.

• Settled in northeastern Arizona.

• Occupied true adobe houses in about the twelfth century, founding cities such as Oraibi and Mesa Verde.

• The Hopi were farmers (corn, squash, beans, cotton, TOBACCO) despite their arid land. The Hopi practiced irrigation on their terraced fields. They developed rich and complex religious and cultural systems

Horse

With the Cortés expedition of 1519, horses once again touched Mexican soil. After thousands of years of absence, the species returned. In 1540, Francisco Vasquez de CORONADO explored northward leading a small group. He reached what is today Kansas. Even though he did not find gold or wealth, he encountered the Wichita Indians. They were greatly frightened by the sight of these unknown animals; but their fear was rapidly replaced by curiosity, and the Comanche were the first to acquire horses by trading slaves with the Spanish. In 1680, a number of horses escaped from the Spanish and spread throughout the borders of New Mexico and Texas where they proliferated rapidly. They then flooded the Great Plains where successive Indian tribes integrated them into their lifestyles. This century-long migration transformed the species: the Andalusian horse (Iberian, also called Barb) was an off-shoot of the Arab and Numid breeds. Delicate and spirited, they found themselves confronted with the trials of winter and attacks from predators. The price of such freedom was that natural selection favored the strongest; the species lost around an inch at the withers and was rewarded with a new name: MUSTANG (from the Spanish *mestengos*, meaning "lost"). According to contemporary estimates, there were more than 2 million horses running free on the Great Plains in 1800.

Seeing the Spanish and believing that the man and horse became one, like the centaurs of mythology, the Indians used this "imported ally" very quickly to their benefit. From 1700 on, some Indians used horses for HUNTING bison; they replaced dogs for towing travois and facilitated winter migrations. An admirable friendship was established between man and animal: The Indian selected his future steed from the herds that would pass close by his encampment.

93

HOUSING

1 - Papago
2 - Seminole
3 - Kutchin
4 - Mandan
5 - Wichita
6 - Ojibwa
7 - Sauk
8 - Haida

He captured the horse, trained it, spoke to it, gave it a great deal of care, and often slept with it under the same shelter. Among all the horsemen, the COMANCHES are known as the most accomplished. They were nicknamed "the Cossacks of the New World" and were simultaneously both exceptional riders and trainers. Certain tribes distinguished themselves with their aptitude for breeding, such as the Nez Perce, to whom is due the credit for the famed Appaloosas of the spotted coat.

Indispensable for hunting or war, the horse is also seen as proof of wealth: Some Comanche tribes with 2,000 members possessed more than 15,000 horses, and the chiefs could personally own more than 1,000. In the Assiniboine tribe, the average was two horses per warrior and increased to 50 for the Nez Perce. Other tribes, such as the Crow, did not hesitate to augment their own herds by stealing their neighbors' animals.

Houma

• Their name means "red."
• Language: Muskogean.
• Settled in the bayous of Louisiana, to the east of the mouth of the Mississippi and near the sources of the Red River.
• The Houma were peaceful farmers and had developed music, dance, and sports activities. Their war emblem was a crayfish with its claws extended,

and the eagle feather was their symbol of peace.
• The Houma were visited by Cavelier La Salle and then Iberville and were in ongoing contact with the French. They are still influenced by Cajun culture. There are approximately 15,000 Houma today, and they have formed the United Houma Nation with a tribal council recognized by the State of Louisiana.

Housing

Depending on the type of dwelling, women (skin-covered tipis on the plains, forest shelters made from birch bark, etc.) and more often men (Iroquois longhouses, igloos, Hopi

Osages

Iroquois

villages) built housing. Using the available materials, the architecture of Indian houses was always well-adapted to the way of life (sedentary or nomadic) and the climate.

Hunkpapa

Their name may mean "those who camp apart" or "at the edges of the circle." The Hunkpapa were a subgroup of the Teton Sioux. At the end of the nineteenh century, their most famous representatives were the chiefs BIG FOOT and SITTING BULL.

Hunt

Throughout their history, the Indians showed that they knew how to hunt responsibly, only killing the number of animals necessary and sufficient for their needs. Early environmentalists viewed animals with the same respect that they accorded to any being that breathed the same air, drank from the same waters,

and shared the same prairies and forests. They admired the animals' different strengths, their might, or their bravery; hunting expeditions were preceded by rituals, to ensure success as well as to honor their future victims. Their prey was numerous and diverse: BISON, various types of *Cervidae* (such as CARIBOU, WAPITI, various deer such as fallow deer and others), BEAR, rabbit and many types of birds (DUCKS, geese, etc.).

Other prey were also pursued but for reasons other than their meat: EAGLES for their feathers, PORCUPINE for their quills, and, wolves, beavers, otter, ermine, prairie dogs, and others for their fur. From adolescence on, the younger members of the tribes participated in hunting expeditions with their elders. Before the arrival of the Europeans, the Indians had only primitive weapons. Great herds of

97

long horn bison—a species that is closely related to bison, but now extinct—were hunted using a simple and efficient technique: waving weapons and flaming torches, the men would scare a herd and guide it toward a natural ditch or cliff. The animals would fall over the edge and were finished off by other hunters. A site dating from 8,500 B.C. discovered near the town of Kit Carson, Colorado, is evidence of this method.

When the animals were in small groups, the Indians would hide under bison pelts, allowing them to get close to their prey and to shoot their arrows from a close distance. They would also hide under wolf pelts: the bison were used to having this predator nearby and this helped the hunter to avoid causing a male to charge before being able to shoot his arrow. The hunters of the Southeast used the same technique to hunt deer.

In winter, small bands of Chippewa hunters would manage to surprise bison, caribou and moose who were partially immobilized in the deep snow. This approach was made possible due to their use of snowshoes. The "animal drive" was a method used by the Hurons from current-day Ontario to trap deer. The hunters would fan out in a semicircle and push the creature toward an enclosed area where it was slain. The Paiute in Nevada used a similar technique to hunt rabbits. The Cherokee hunted small game with blowguns that had a range of 65 feet (20 meters). In the north, the Inuits hunted SEAL by finding the holes in the ice where the animal came to breathe. With the arrival of the Europeans, the Indians acquired two new tools that radically changed their hunting methods: firearms and horses. The bison hunt, in particular, was changed: from high on their mount, the Dakota, Kiowa, Cheyenne, and Pawnee no longer needed to resort to ruses to get close to the herd. Galloping next to the bison, they would discharge their arrows with precision. With a gun, they were even more efficient. Regretfully, they were no longer the only ones on the hunt, and, within several decades, in the nineteenth century, the huge herd of bison that had populated the Great Plains had been eradicated.

Hupa

• Their name comes from the Yurok's corruption of the name of the Hoopa Valley in California, in which the Hupa lived.

• Language: Athabascan.

• The Hupa settled in the valleys of the Trinity River and the New River, and the lower branch of the Klamath River in the Hoopa Valley.

• Their villages were a collection of small houses made of thuya or CEDAR wood arranged around the sweat lodge. The women were skilled basket weavers, and the men were adept at wood sculpting. Hupa society was founded on the richness of its individuals and was governed by a complex code: their various conflicts were resolved through compromise and restitution.

• As the Hupa were isolated in valleys, they had contact with whites relatively late, in about 1850. Out of concern for avoiding the loss of the Hupa, the U.S. government set up a reservation for them in 1864.

• Estimated at 1,000 in the middle of the nineteenth century, the Hupa population has probably doubled today.

Huron

- The Huron called themselves *Wendat*, "people of the peninsula." They were also called *Guyandot* or *Wyandot*. CHAMPLAIN's companions called them the Huron, after the French word *hure*, meaning "boar's head," in reference to their bristly hair styles.
- Language: Iroquoian.
- Settled between Lake Huron and Lake Ontario.
- The Huron were farmers (corn, beans, sunflowers), fishermen, and hunters. They traded furs and tobacco. Their villages were placed near a lake or river. They built long houses made of elm bark.
- The Huron were divided into four clans (Rock, Cord, Bear, and Deer), and were organized into a confederacy. Some Huron were converted to Christianity by missionaries and the Huron allied themselves with the French. Their enemies the IROQUOIS, alongside the English and the Dutch, used this as a pretext for almost completely annihilating them in 1648.
- Today, descendants of the Huron live on the Wyandot reservation in Oklahoma. Another community exists in Lorette, Quebec.

Husk Face Society

For the Iroquois, the job of the Husk Face Society was to protect the crops, predict the abundance of harvests, and help in bringing many children. The society's rituals took place in the middle of winter: the men of the SOCIETY danced from house to house to sweep the ashes out of the home. All of the men wore masks made of corn husks, made into the shape of faces.

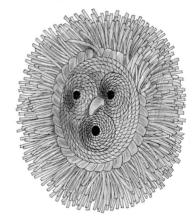

I-J

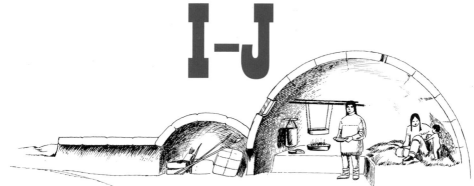

Igloo

A shelter that the INUITS built to withstand the cold and snowstorms of the polar winter. Made of blocks of ice arranged in an ascending spiral, the igloo is ventilated by a small hole in the roof which is covered with a piece of seal skin.

Illinois

• Their name is a French deformation of their Indian name *Illiniwek*, meaning "man."
• Language: Algonquian.
• Populated the northern part of the present-day state of Illinois, to which they gave their name.
• The Illinois hunted bison and were semi-nomadic. They made up a confederation of tribes: the Peorias, Kaskaskias, Tamaroas, Cahokias, Michigameas, and Moingwenas.
• Allied with the French, they were crushed by the Iroquois in 1684. The great Ottawa chief PONTIAC was killed by an Illinois in 1769. As revenge, the Kickapoos launched a campaign of

extermination: there were only a few hundred Illinois survivors.
• After their land was sold, they went into exile in Kansas. In 1854, a treaty brought the Peoria, Kaskaskia and the Miami, Wea, and Piankashaw tribes together on a reservation in Oklahoma.
• There were approximately 10,000 Illinois in 1680, but the Illinois then almost disappeared, with 180 remaining in 1937. Today, there are probably almost 2,000 Illinois.

101

Indian Reorganization Act

A reform launched in 1934 by John Collier, the Commissioner of Indian Affairs under President Franklin D. Roosevelt. The act, also referred to as the Wheeler-Howard Act, aimed to put an end to the looting of RESERVATIONS and the despoiling of lands. Industrial facilities were encouraged on the reservations, and SCHOOLS and health centers were opened.

Indian Rights Association

An association founded in 1882 by John Welch. While agitating for the rights of Indian peoples, the association participated in mobilizing the elite of the east, following massacres against the Cheyennes (1878) and the Poncas (1879).

Inglaki

• Name given by the Inuits, who had supplanted them on the Alaska coast, and which means "They have lice." The Russians gave this name to all the Athabascans in Alaska. Their real name was *Kaiyukhotana*.
• Language: Athabascan.
• Inhabited the lower parts of the Yukon and Kuskokwin Rivers.
• Only censuses after the nineteenth century can be considered trustworthy, but they include all of the Athabascans of the region (Ahtena, Koyukon, Kutchin, Tanana and Tanaina): 4,935 individuals in 1930.

Interbreeding

Interbreeding between Europeans and Indians began in the sixteenth century, when French and English colonists arrived in Canada. The fur trade led trappers, especially those of French origin, to immerse themselves in the Indian world. The result of this was an interracial population who were more economically powerful than numerous. The phenomenon of interbreeding affected Canada more than the future United States.

The interracial population relied completely on the trade in animal skins; the approximately 30,000 interracial persons in the Canadian West were hard hit by the disappearance of the bison herd and the building of the Canadian Pacific Railway.

In 1885, in an effort to protect their interests, the interracial population formed a provisional government of Saskatchewan under the direction of Louis Riel and mustered a force of 700 men, bolstered by Cree and Assiniboine Indians. From March to July 1885, the regular Canadian forces came up against the immigrants who were finally defeated. Louis Riel surrendered, was convicted, and was hanged despite a tide of popular opinion in his favor. Very harsh penalties were levied against the other insurgents.

Interbreeding between whites and Indians in the United States and Canada remains impossible to quantify. Today, censuses do not make any effort to determine the degree of interbreeding between the populations. Interbreeding is common among Cherokees and marginal among the Navajo, but it nevertheless exists and slowly plays a role in changing the dominant white world's attitude toward the "first Americans."

Inuit

• Their name means "men" in their language.
• Language: Eskimo-Aleut.
• We can identify three main zones in the Inuit world, which extends over more than 4,000 miles from west to east:
– to the west, the entire Alaskan coast, the Aleutian Islands to the mouth of the Mackenzie River. The Aleut, the most southern, made their houses from wood and cetacean bones; the most northern lived in half-buried shelters covered with earth.

– at the western edge of the Inuit world, in Greenland, the Inuit lived in stone dwellings and hunted whales in the Davis Strait. From the tenth century on, they were in contact with VIKINGS; this relationship gave rise to a profitable trade in skins, furs, and ivory between Greenland and Northern Europe.
– in the central region, from Mackenzie to the northern edge of Labrador, including all the islands and territories around the northern part of Hudson Bay. In these areas, the Inuit had to confront the rigors of a hostile environment and had to fight incessantly for

Copper

Mackenzie

103

their survival in vast areas of ice blasted by polar winds.

• The Inuit traveled in bands of forty to fifty individuals, meaning ten to fifteen hunters. They had no chiefs, but for HUNTING, the most experienced hunter was often designated as the leader. The only Inuit with distinct powers was the shaman. The shaman was a hunter and had children like the other members of the community, and he could communicate with the SPIRITS; the shaman also had the power to take care of the sick, meaning the power to heal.

Iowa

• From the Dakota word *Ayuhwa*: "those who sleep." May also come from *ai'yuwe*, "zucchini."
• Language: Siouan.
• According to French traders, the Iowa were skilled traders and farmers. They measured their wealth in BISON skins and CALUMETS, of which they were renowned as sculptors.
• The Iowa had contact with the French (Marquette in 1674, Le Moyne d'Iberville in 1702). In 1804, they were encountered by the LEWIS and CLARK

Greenland

Baffin

expedition, then many times by George CATLIN, who painted some splendid portraits of their chiefs. The Iowa were a peaceful people and integrated into reservations in Kansas (1836) and then in Oklahoma (1883).

- There were 1,100 Iowa in 1760. In 1990, there were 300 Iowa in Oklahoma, 400 in Kansas and 200 in Nebraska.

Iroquois

- Their name comes from the Algonquian word *Irinakhoiw*, which designated the Senecas and meant "true snakes."
- The Iroquois called themselves *Hodinonhsioni*: "people of the large house."
- The League of Five Nations included, from west to east: The **Seneca**, a Dutch and English mispronunciation of their name *Tsonondowaka* ("mountain people"); the **Cayuga** ("people of the wetlands"); the **Onondaga** ("on the top of the hill"); the **Oneida** ("people of the upright stone"); and the **Mohawk** or

Iroquoian

See Languages, pg. 14.

105

exhausted. A typical Iroquois "long house" measured 65 to 98 feet (20 to 30 meters) in length, and housed up to twenty families.

- The Iroquois were sedentary farmers (corn, squash and beans, which they nicknamed "the three sisters"). They were also remarkable hunters and implacable warriors. The Iroquois worshiped a complex group of animals, plants, and natural forces dominated by the Great Spirit, or *Orenda*.

- Iroquois WOMEN owned all the property, in particular the large houses. They carried out the harvests and stored food reserves in silos dug into the ground. The tribe was organized around the women's lineage.

- The Great Council included fifty sachems: eight Seneca, ten Cayuga, fourteen Onondaga, nine Oneida and nine Mohawk. In fact, only eight Mohawk participated, since no one replaced HIAWATHA, who inspired the League. The council's decisions were controlled by the women who, when necessary, didn't hold back from expressing their disapproval or from disowning or replacing a chief.

"man-eaters." The Iroquois called themselves *Kaniengehaga* ("people of the place of the flint").

- The League became the Confederacy of Six Nations in 1722, with the arrival of the **Tuscarora** ("hemp gatherers").
- Language: Iroquoian.
- Settled on the southern shores of Lake Ontario, in large villages surrounded by fences.
- The Iroquois cleared and cultivated the land immediately around their villages. Every 15 to 20 years, the village moved after the area around it was

representative of the YAHI tribe was discovered living alone on his tribe's land, near Mount Lassen in northeastern California. After attracting the attention of scientists, Ishi (meaning "man" in his language) learned more than 600 English words and provided numerous pieces of information on his language, his way of life, and his fishing and hunting techniques. Ishi had a peaceful temperament, was shocked by the white world, of which he had been unaware, and overcame his fear of crowds. He had never been in the presence of more than twenty or thirty people at the same time. Ishi, the last witness of a lost world, died of tuberculosis.

• Until the end of the eighteenth century, the Iroquois participated in all conflicts. Allied with the English against the French, their actions were decisive. Under the direction of Joseph BRANT, they remained faithful to their allies against the American insurgents (only the Oneidas chose neutrality). Their villages were destroyed in 1779, at the end of their defeat.

• The Iroquois were brought together on many reservations in New York state, and also in Wisconsin (Oneida), Oklahoma (Seneca), and Canada. There were about 49,000 Iroquois according to the 1990 census.

Itazipchos

"Without bows." A subgroup of the Teton Sioux.

Jackson
Andrew (1767-1845)

He participated in the Revolutionary War, served as both a senator and a judge, and once again took up arms in 1812. After many victories over the SEMINOLE Indians who were allies of the English (1818), Jackson successfully defended New Orleans. He became governor of Florida in 1821; then he became a senator again. He ran for president in 1825. After being beaten by John Quincy Adams, he won the election in 1828 and was reelected in 1832.

Ishi
(circa 1860-1916)

In August, 1911, an Indian who was approximately 50 years old and the last

As the seventh president of the United States, Jackson was an energetic diplomat; he reduced the public debt and made sound decisions regarding finances.

Jefferson
Thomas (1743-1826)

A great artist of American independence, he held many important positions before becoming the head of the Republican Party, whose agenda included allegiance with France. He was elected as vice president in 1797 and as the third president of the United States in 1800. Jefferson was reelected in 1804 but refused to run a third time. Jefferson was a good administrator and a friend and disciple of the French philosophers; he was the first person to apply the humanist principles of the Age of Light. He decided to purchase Louisiana from France in 1803 and was a proponent of the LEWIS and CLARK expedition, which initiated the colonization of the West.

Johnson
William (1715-1774)

Johnson was a general of Irish origin whose actions were decisive during the French-English War. Having lived among the Mohawks, he knew their language well and married the daughter of a great chief, then the sister of Joseph BRANT. Emboldened by this collaboration with the Iroquois, Johnson succeeded in making them the implacable adversaries of the French.

Joliet
Louis (1645-1700)

Joliet was an explorer born in Quebec. In 1672, along with the Jesuit priest Jacques MARQUETTE, he undertook a voyage to find the Great River that the Indians spoke about, hoping to travel down it and reach the Pacific. Via Lake Michigan, Green Bay, and the Fox and Illinois Rivers, Joliet and Marquette found the Great River (meaning the MISSISSIPPI) and crossed the center of the continent, arriving at its mouth on the Gulf of Mexico.

Julius II
(1443-1513)

Julius II was pope from 1503 to 1513 and organized the Fifth Council of the Lateran. After he was informed of the way in which the Spanish conquistadors had enslaved the inhabitants of the New World, Julis II proclaimed in 1512 that the Indians were the children of Adam and Eve and as such should be treated with humanity and respect.

K

Kachina

sponded to a mask that dancers wore during ceremonies. To help CHILDREN memorize each spirit and learn about how to worship it, adults made Kachina dolls for the children out of wood and fabric. Missionaries tried to forbid the product of these types of objects, which they judged to be pagan, but the Hopis continued to make them in secret.

Kainah

See Blackfeet.

Kalapooya

For the Indians of the Southwest, particularly the HOPI and the ZUNI, the term "Kachina" was used for the various spirits and invisible forces that nourished and protected humans. The Kachinas could help the tribe obtain a good harvest, keep war at bay, and make rain fall. The Kachinas came out of the ground between the winter solstice and the summer solstice and then returned to the "underworld." Each spirit corre-

- The meaning of their name is unknown.
- They spoke a Kalapooian dialect that was common to all of the bands and tribes in the region (Ahantchuyuk, Atfalati, Chelamela, Chepenafa, Luckiamute, Santiam, Yamel, and Yoncalla).
- Lived along the Willamette River in present-day Oregon.
- The entire Kalapooian group had a population of 3,000 in 1780 and 130 in 1905.

Kalispel
- Their name comes from the word *camas*. They were also called the *Pend d'Oreilles*, meaning "hangs from ears" in French, for their custom of hanging large shells from their ears.
- Language: Salishan.
- Inhabited the far northwest of the present-day state of Wyoming (around Lake Pend Oreille and along the lower part of the Clark's Fork River).
- The Kalispel were driven off their land by the construction of the railroad (1883) and the discovery of tin mines.
- There were 1,200 Kalispel in 1780, and there are 200 today on a reservation in Washington State, near the Spokane reservation.

Kane
Paul (1810-1871)
A Canadian painter, Kane began his career as a decorator. After being deeply impressed by the work of George CATLIN, he left to explore Northwestern Canada in 1845 and painted the same types of scenes. After traveling for 4 years by canoe and dogsled, he came back with 700 drawings of some eighty tribes. In Toronto, he completed his paintings and wrote a memoir of his trip, called *Among the Indians of North America*, published in 1859.

Kansas
- The Kansas were also called the *Kaw*, meaning "south wind."

- Language: Siouan.
- The Kansas settled in the eastern part of the state that today bears their name and observed a semi-nomadic way of life that was identical to that of the other Dhegihas tribes.
- They gave extreme attention to spiritual life. Puberty rites included, for boys, the experience of dreams and visions that determined their future. Funeral ceremonies were long and carefully codified.
- The Kansas were undoubtedly in contact with Coronado from 1541 on. Marquette met them in 1673. They were sent to a reservation in Topeka,

Kansas

Kansas, in 1846, and their territory was progressively reclaimed by the federal government. They were then moved to Oklahoma and a new reservation near that of the Osage.
• In Oklahoma, there were 3,000 Kansas in 1780 and 543 in 1985.

Karankawa

• A group of many tribes sharing the same dialect and located on the coast of the Gulf of Mexico in the state of Texas, between the cities of Galveston and Corpus Christi.
• Their small communities were in contact many times with the whites in the sixteenth and seventeenth centuries: They took in Nunez Cabeza de Vaca and were visited by Cavelier de La Salle and by the Spanish. According to their neighbors, the Karankawa voluntarily committed cannibalism.
• There were 2,800 Karankawa in 1690, but they disappeared in the centuries that followed.

Karok

• Their name probably came from *karuk*, meaning "upriver people."
• Language: Hokan.
• The Karok lived along the middle part of the Klamath River.
• They were hunters and fishermen, and their history is very similar to that of the Yuroks, whose reservation they share.
• There were 1,500 Karok in 1770. Today, there are probably about 2,000.

Kaska

See Nahane.

Kaskaskia

See Illinois.

Kawchottine

• Their name meant "people of the great hares."
• Language: Athabascan.
• The Kawchottine inhabited the west and north of Great Bear Lake in Canada's Northern Territories.

Karok

• There were 750 Kawchottine in 1670 and 467 in 1858.

Kayak

See Boats.

Keokuk

(1780-1848)

This SAUK chief supported the young American nation during the War of 1812 against the English. Keokuk was extremely courageous and had excellent political sense; in 1832 he opposed the war that BLACK HAWK began. Unlike Black Hawk, Keokuk understood that his people had to abandon the land of his birth (Illinois) for less-coveted regions (present-day Iowa). Today, a city in Iowa bears his name.

Kickapoo

• Their name comes from *Kiwegapan*, meaning "he stands there." The Plains Indians called them "Deer Eaters," and the Hurons called them *Ontarahronon*, "people of the lake."

• Language: Algonquian.

• Settled at the southern end of the western shore of Lake Michigan.

• Formidable warriors, the Kickapoo had the reputation of being "handsome, brave and very independent." They were divided into clans (Eagle, Bear, Fox, Water, and Thunder).

• Marquette and Joliet met them in 1672. The Kickapoo participated in the

Kickapoos

PONTIAC revolt of 1763, the Maumee's revolt against the Americans in 1790, then TECUMSEH's revolt. They also had an important part in the insurrection led by the Sauk chief, BLACK HAWK, in 1832. They were sent away to the south, and settled in Texas with the Delaware and the Cherokees. The Kickapoo allied themselves with the Mexicans in their attempt to reclaim Texas in 1839. Some of the Kickapoo moved to Mexico in order to protect the border from Apache and Comanche incursions.
• There is a reservation for the Mexican Kickapoo in Oklahoma, with 700 residents, and one in Kansas, with approximately 2,000 inhabitants.

King Philip
See Metacom.

Kiowa
• The name Kiowa comes from their name for themselves, *Ka-i-gwy*, meaning "Dominating People."
• Language: Kiowan, a linguistic isolate characterized by stifled sounds.
• In the middle of the eighteenth century, the Kiowa occupied a territory that included parts of the states of Oklahoma, Kansas, Colorado, and Texas.
• They were nomadic bison hunters, excellent horseback riders, and somber and solidly built people. The Kiowa tribe is the only tribe to have kept a record of its history using PICTOGRAMS painted on animal skins (1832–1892).

• Before the eighteenth century, the Kiowa occupied a territory located in Montana, along the Yellowstone River (which resulted in their very friendly ties with the Crows). As soon as they had horses available, they migrated to the south while hunting bison. In 1804 Lewis and Clark identified their location as being along the North Platte River. After reaching Oklahoma, they formed an alliance with their former enemies the Comanche. Considered as the most aggressive of the Plains Indians, they were well armed and well organized, and proved to be indomitable adversaries for the American colonists.
• There were 2,000 Kiowa in 1780, and 9,400 in 1990, in Oklahoma. A Kiowa Great Council still heads the tribe.

Kiowa

113

Kiowa-Apache

• The name designates a tribe of Athabascan origin and language, which integrated into the Kiowa community undoubtedly since the eighteenth century.
• They called themselves *Nadinshadina,* "our people."
• The French called them the *Gattackas,* and the Pawnees referred to the Kiowas as *Taguis,* and to the others as *Kaskias,* "bad hearts," or Prairie Apaches.

Kiowan

See Languages, pg. 15.

Kiva

Partially underground, the kiva was a place of prayer, and a council chamber for the HOPI and ZUNI. The kiva was large enough to accommodate the members of various clans. A small opening in the ground represented the bath that people took to reach the surface of the earth at the time of creation. The opening in the roof was larger and symbolized access to the current world. It also held a ladder, by which people could enter the kiva.

Klallam

• From *Clallam,* meaning "powerful people."
• Language: Salishan.
• Inhabited the southern tip of Vancouver Island and the southern coast of the Strait of Juan de Fuca.
• There were 2,000 Klallam in 1780 and 764 in 1937.

Klamath

• Their name is of unknown origin and was used by other tribes near the Columbia River. The Klamath called themselves *Maklak,* "people," or *Eukshikni maklak,* "people of the lakes."
• Dialect: Lutuamian, shared with the Modoc.
• They lived near the northern shore of Lake Klamath (in southern Oregon) and the basins of the Williamson and Sprague Rivers.
• They existed by hunting (fallow deer, birds) and gathering (wild berries, pine nuts). They carried out raids, after 1849, against miners, but were subjugated by the end of the Civil War.
• There were 800 Klamath in 1780 and approximately 3,500 in 1990. The Klamath have formed a very prosperous

Klondike

A tributary of the Yukon River in the present-day state of Alaska. The confluence zone was inhabited by the Tutchone. The region was famous for the discovery of GOLD in Rabbit Creek on August 17, 1896. This event caused the rush of tens of thousands of adventurers, and "mushroom cities" such as Dawson (which had a population of 40,000 at the height of the gold rush) sprung up. It also caused the disappearance of the Indians who lived there.

community since coming together with the Modoc and the Yahooskin.

Klikitat

• Their name comes from a Chinook term meaning "beyond," referring to the waterfalls on the Columbia River.
• Language: Sahahptian.
• Settled along the lower part of the Columbia River, the border between the present-day states of Washington and Oregon.
• The Klikitat distinguished themselves through their skill for commercial trading at the axis of the Columbia River, between the tribes from the coast and those from the interior. The women were experts at BASKET WEAVING, making large baskets decorated with geometric patterns.
• There were 1700 Klikitat in 1780 and 405 in 1910.

Kootenai

• A corruption of one of their names, *Kutonaga*, by their enemies the Blackfeet. The Nez-Perces and the Salishs called them "people of the water."
• Their language is a linguistic isolate.
• The Kootenai settled in southeastern British

Kootenai

115

Columbia, northwestern Montana, and northeastern Washington.
• They were enemies of the Blackfeet, but their relationships with the whites were fairly cordial.
• Estimated at 1,200 in 1780, some Kootenai live today on a reservation in Canada (549 people in 1967) and some in Idaho (123 in 1985).

Koyukon

• A contraction of *Koyukukhotana,* "people of the river."
• Language: Athabascan.
• Lived along the Koyukuk River, a tributary of the Yukon River in Western Alaska.
• There were 1,500 Koyukon in 1740 and 940 in 1890.

Kutchin

• Etymologically name means "people." The Kutchin were also called the "Loucheux."
• Language: Athabascan.
• Their region was between the high valley of the Yukon and the mouth of the Mackenzie River in Alaska.
• Despite being very hospitable, the Kutchin had the reputation of being more aggressive than the other Athabascans. They were great caribou hunters, lake and river anglers and animal trappers.

• In fact, the Kutchin were a group of tribes that each had their own territory: the Kutcha, Dihai, Tennuth, Takkuth, and Tatlit.
• Alexander MACKENZIE met them in 1789. Their relationships with the white world were then established because of the Hudson Bay Company. The discovery of GOLD in the Klondike Valley in 1896 disrupted their free and nomadic way of life.

Kutchin snowshoes

- Their population was evaluated at 1,200 people in 1936.

Kwakiutl

- Their name has two possible meanings: "smoke of the world," or more likely "beach on the north side of the river."

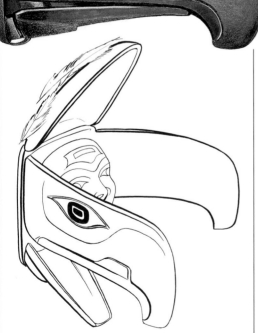

Kwakiutl mask with movable parts

- Language: Wakashan (second division with the Bella Bellas).
- The Kwakiutl occupied the coasts of the Queen Charlotte Strait and the northern part of Vancouver Island. The Kwakiutl were renowned navigators, DEER and CARIBOU hunters, and, above all, fishermen. They excelled at trapping the salmon that swam up the rivers each year and used nets, harpoons, landing nets, and wicker grids that they set up at the tops of waterfalls.
- The Kwakiutl lived in large cedar houses that housed many families. They made clothing and mats by mixing the interior bark of red cedars with skins and furs.
- After Bodega passed through in 1775, they welcomed explorers and traders, who they supplied with furs and otter skins. They managed to preserve their culture despite the efforts of missionaries.
- There were 8,000 Kwakiutl in the middle of the nineteenth century and approximately 4,000 in 1990.

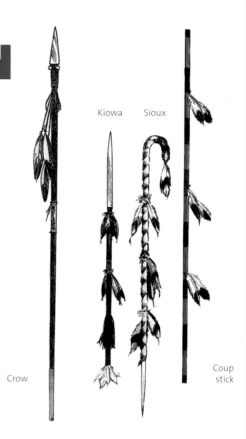

Kiowa   Sioux

Crow

Coup stick

Lacrosse

See Games.

Lake

• Tribes that were thus nicknamed because they settled along the Columbia River where it crosses the Arrow Lakes near the present-day border between the United States and Canada (on the Canadian side). Their true name was the *Senijextees* (meaning unknown).
• Language: Salishan.
• There were 500 Lake in 1780 and 785 in 1910.

Lakota

See Dakota.

Lances

Without a doubt, the oldest WEAPON, the lance, completed the attack arsenal of Indian warriors; equipped with a point made of bone or carved stone, the lance is a throwing weapon, identical to the javelin. Approximately 6.5 feet (2 meters) in length, the lance, unlike the TOMAHAWK, is more used for hunting

than for wartime combat. With the appearance of the HORSE in the Indian world, the lance was adopted by mounted soldiers and reached almost 10 feet (3 meters) in length. The point was made of iron, salvaged from weapons taken from the Whites (knives, swords, etc). The lance was frequently decorated with FEATHERS, pieces of cloth, leather, or fur.

To the Sioux, the crooked lance, a sort of large cane with a pointed end, was more a sign of dignity than a weapon meant for combat, but as

118

necessity was the mother of invention, the crooked lance also served to deliver BLOWS to enemies.

Las Casas
Bartolomé de (1474-1566)

A Spanish prelate and the son of one of Christopher Columbus's companions, Las Casas devoted his life to pleading the cause of the Indians who had been reduced to slavery by the Spanish in their *encomiendas*. From the island of Haiti, he crossed the ocean twelve times to go to the court of Madrid in order to defend the people he sought to protect by advocating new and more humane laws (1542). Charles V and Philip II called him "The universal protector of all the Indians." To Las Casas we owe *A very brief account of the devastation of the Indies*, in which he denounced the atrocities committed by the conquistadors. His writings found little support with the colonists, but the church authorities were more attentive, and Pope PAUL III intervened on behalf of the Indians (1537).

Laudonnière
René de (died 1572)

He was directed by Admiral de Coligny to found a colony for persecuted Protestants in Florida (1562). He constructed Fort Caroline on the St. John River. After losing the support of the Timucua Indians because of poor decisions, Laudonnière and his companions were attacked by the Spanish on September 20, 1565. Laudonnière succeeded in escaping and was vindicated by the expedition of Dominique de Gourgues in 1568.

La Vérendrye
Pierre Gaultier de (1685-1749)

A French Canadian explorer born in Trois-Rivières. He combined fur trading with the discovery of new regions, and carried out, with his sons, many expeditions to Lake Winnipeg, then to the upper Missouri and Mandan villages. His sons continued exploring, reaching the BLACK HILLS.

Lewis
Meriwether (1774-1809)

A Captain in the U.S. Army, then President JEFFERSON's private secretary, he met William CLARK in St. Louis in 1804 for an expedition that aimed to find the best path to cross the Rockies and reach the Pacific. Along the way, he also wanted to create cordial relationships with the Indian tribes that he met. The expedition, which included about fifty people, was guided by a Shoshone, SACAJAWEA ("bird woman"), and the trapper Toussaint Charbonneau, and found new, totally untouched territories. After 2 years and

119

5 months of travel by foot, horse, and canoe, covering more than 9,320 miles (15,000 kilometers) and experiencing both suffering and amazement, the Lewis and Clark expedition came back to the east without having fired a shot against the Indians. There was only one death on the expedition, caused by appendicitis.

Lilloet

• Their name meant "wild onion."
• Language: Salishan.
• They lived in the area delimited to the east by the Bridge River and Lake Anderson, and to the west by the Lilloet River in British Columbia.
• The Lilloet were hit particularly hard by the smallpox epidemic of 1863. There were 4,000 Lilloets in 1780, 1,600 in 1904 and 2,300 in 1967.

Little Big Horn

The Little Big Horn River is a tributary of the Big Horn River, which flows into the Yellowstone River in the Southeastern part of the present-day state of Montana. In the valley of the Little Big Horn on June 25, 1876, the famous battle between General CUSTER's seventh cavalry regiment and many thousands of Sioux, Cheyenne, and Arapahoe warriors took place. The rout of the "blue shirts" and Custer's death generated considerable emotion in the United States. This was a glorious day for the Indians. Little Big Horn

represented the beginning of their end, as the Americans continually sought to take revenge for this insult.

Little Crow
(1820-1863)

A Sioux chief (of the Santee people). Exasperated by the broken promises of the colonists and white traders, he stirred up a revolt in August 1862 in Minnesota. Little Crow also blamed the government for purposefully depriving his people of food by withholding food that they had promised the Indians in exchange for the sale of their lands. After many extremely bloody raids,

The Yellowstone River valley, Wyoming

Little Crow was killed in an act of treachery by a gunshot to the back.

Little Turtle
(1752–1812)

An exceptionally brave and intelligent MIAMI chief, Little Turtle worked to establish the Ohio River as a division line between the Indians and the whites. As the leader of the Miami, Shawnee, and Potawatomi warriors, he was the winner of many conflicts, including the battle of Wabash against the American forces of General Saint Clair on November 4, 1791.

Little Wolf
(1820-1904)

A CHEYENNE chief, Little Wolf is known for two extraordinary acts. In 1874 he went to Washington and met President Ulysses GRANT; Little Wolf proposed to Grant to accept 1,000 white women into his tribe in order to facilitate the integra-

tion of Indians into the American nation. In 1878 he obtained a reservation for the Northern Cheyennes; the reservation was not in dry and arid Oklahoma, but on their own territory in Montana. Leading a group of 400 people in the cold and snow, Little Wolf began a "long march" of over 3,000 miles (5,000 kilometers).

Luiseño

• Their name came from the San Luis Rey de Francia mission. They were also called Ghechams or Khechams.
• Language: Shoshonean.
• Lived in Southwestern California.
• There were 4,000 Luiseño in 1770; 1,150 in 1885; and 2,700 in 1985.

Lynx

The lynx's natural habitat included all of the deep forests in present-day Canada. The lynx is an excellent swimmer, and its population density reaches a critical point every 10 years, as does that of its preferred prey, the snowshoe hare, which is white in winter and brown in summer.

M

Machapunga

- Their name means "bad dust" or "muddy," undoubtedly referring to the swampy areas in which they lived.
- Language: Algonquian.
- Lived along the Atlantic coast, in the wetlands of present-day North Carolina, bounded by Albemarle Sound to the north and Pamlico sound to the south.
- Considered to be the descendants of the SECOTANS. They were one of the rare Indian peoples to practice circumcision.
- There were 1,200 Machapunga in 1600, and about 100 at the end of the eighteenth century.

Mackenzie
Sir Alexander (1755-1820)

Mackenzie was a Scottish traveler who explored the northern regions of North America and reached the Arctic Ocean on behalf of the North West Company. Mackenzie set off in 1789 with a small group of Indians aboard birch bark canoes; he discovered the river that today bears his name and then crossed the Rockies via the Columbia River, heading for the Pacific, which he reached in 1793.

Mahican

- According to certain interpretations, their name means "the wolves." Others believe that it means "tide," in reference to the movement of the waters of the Hudson River.
- Language: Algonquian.
- The Mahican settled on the banks of the Hudson River.
- They were hunters, farmers, and fishermen; their way of life was close to that of the Delawares and the Mohegan.

123

• At war against the Mohawks for control of fur trading on the Hudson. From the beginning of the eighteenth century on, English settlements drove the Mahican off their land, while SMALLPOX and tuberculosis severely affected them. Like the majority of Algonquin, they sided with the French. Some Mahican fought under the orders of General LaFayette during the Revolutionary War.

• Two Mahican groups, the Stockbridge-Munsee, live on a reservation in Wisconsin.

Maidu

• Their name means "person" in their language. Like their neighbors the Paiute, they were nicknamed "diggers" by the whites because they sought out roots to complete their berry- and acorn-based diet.

• Language: Penutian.

• The Maidu lived along the upper part of the Feather Rivers, in Plumas County, California.

• There were 9,000 Maidu in 1770, 93 in 1930, and 338 in 1985.

Makah

• Their name meant "people of the cape."

• Language: Wakashan.

• The Makah lived near Cape Flattery (today, the border between the United States and Canada), across from Vancouver Island.

• They practiced gathering and salmon FISHING. They also hunted SEALS and WHALES on the open ocean.

• The Makah were excellent wood artists, whether the task was building their immense houses, their large totem poles, their ocean canoes, or their harpoons.

• Transferred their territory to the U.S. government in 1855. However, they were given a small reservation on the same land in 1893.

• The Makah population was estimated at 2,000 in 1780; today there are approximately 1,500 Makah in Neah Bay.

Malecite

• Their name comes from a Micmac term meaning "bad speaker," which can be interpreted in many ways: either referring to an incorrect language (as compared with the Micmac language) or meaning "liars."

• Language: Algonquian.

• Members of the Wabanaki confederation along with the Micmac, Abenaki, and Penobscot.

• The Malecite were semi-nomadic and existed by HUNTING and FISHING, but they also grew corn. They traded furs with the French.

- Occupied the Saint John River valley in southern New Brunswick before relocating to Quebec.
- There were 800 Malecite in 1600 and 712 in Quebec in 1995.

Mandan

- Their name is a corruption the Dakota term for them, *Mawatani*. They called themselves *Numakaki*, "men."
- Language: Siouan.
- Settled in North Dakota along the Missouri River, between the confluence of the Little Missouri and Heart Rivers. The Mandan lived in houses that could accommodate about thirty people.
- The Mandan came from the Great

Lakes in about the fourteenth century. They were among the first Sioux to settle on the Great Plains. They were visited by LEWIS and CLARK in 1804, then by the painters George Catlin and Karl Bodmer in 1832 and 1833. The smallpox epidemic of 1837 almost eliminated them, leaving only 128 survivors (23 men, 40 women, and 65 children).
- They combined a sedentary farming life (growing corn) with hunting BISON. They were also skilled potters and excellent traders. Their position on the Missouri made their villages places of trade between tribes from the north and south, and later between white and Indian traders who dealt in furs.
- The Mandan practiced complex rituals and ceremonies, notably the *Okeepa* which reenacted the formation of the Earth and the creation of all living beings.
- There were 3,600 Mandan in 1780 and 1,600 in 1837 before the epidemic. In 1990 approximately 1,000 Mandan lived on the Fort Berthold reservation around Lake Sakakawea in North Dakota, along with the Hidatsa and the Arikara.

Mangus Colorado
(1798-1863)

From the Spanish *Mangas coloradas* ("red sleeves"). His real name was Dasoda-Hae, "the one who is seated there." This great APACHE chief wanted to unite all of his people's tribes, and so

125

carried on a constant war, first against the Mexicans, then against the Americans. At the end of his life, he wanted to see peace reestablished, but he was tricked and then killed on the San Carlos reservation after appearing for a peace talk.

Manitou

A misspelling of the Indian name *Manitto*, the Algonquian-language peoples' word for the Great SPIRIT, the power that created and was the master of every living thing on earth. This power, who had magical capabilities, was present to all of the Indian tribes with some variations: The Iroquois called the spirit *Orenda*, the Shoshones *Pokunt*, the Sioux *Wakanda*; the spirit was also called Sulia (Salish), Naulak (Kwakiutl), Tamanoas (Chinook), Tirawa (Pawnee), and Maheo (Cheyenne).

Maple

Three types of maple trees thrived in eastern North America: the silver maple, the red maple, and the sugar maple. The Indians extracted the sugar maple's abundant syrup in the spring; they stored it in birch bark cauldrons and brought it to a boil by putting very hot stones into it. The resulting syrup was an important nutritional supplement for

the Iroquois and the Algonquin of the east. The recipe was passed on to the colonists and remains a much-enjoyed food.

Marquette
Jacques (1637-1675)

Marquette was a French Jesuit born in Laon, France. With Louis JOLIET, he explored the Wisconsin River in 1637. Afterward, the two men went down the Mississippi River, recognizing the confluences of the Missouri and Ohio Rivers along the way. Then, they went upstream on the Illinois River as far as Chicago. Their meetings with the Indians (Fox, Peoria, Illinois) were always peaceful. Marquette's *An Account of the Discovery of Some New Countries and Nations in North America* was published in 1682.

Marriage
See Family.

Massachusetts
- Means "large hill."
- Language: Algonquian.
- They settled on the banks of Massachusetts Bay, on the site of the present-day city of Boston, between the cities of Salem, to the north, and Mansfield, to the south.

- They were undoubtedly visited by John Cabot, then by Captain John SMITH in 1614. The Massachusetts lived in small villages that were well organized according to a strict hierarchy dominated by the chief, or *sachem*.
- The Massachusetts grew beans and peas, hunted deer, and fished in rivers.
- There were 3,000 Massachusetts in 1600. Smallpox epidemics killed 90 percent of the population.

Massassoit

(?–1661)

Massassoit was the legendary chief of the WAMPANOAGS. He is credited with saving the people who arrived on the *Mayflower* by teaching them how to grow corn, a crop that was unknown to the English colonists. He wanted to maintain good relations with the Pilgrim Fathers, and so signed a peace treaty with them in approximately 1621.

Mayflower

On September 6, 1620, the *Mayflower* set off from Plymouth, England. The boat brought 102 colonists, known as the Pilgrim Fathers, to America; they belonged to a Protestant sect that was persecuted in England. The *Mayflower* dropped anchor on December 21, and the exhausted colonists, many suffering from scurvy, founded Plymouth, on Cape Cod Bay in Massachusetts. Before going ashore, they wrote the *Covenant*, the first American Constitution.

Medicine

A misspelling of the Algonquian word *Midewiwin*. To the Indians, this referred to everything mysterious or magical, whether to cure evil or to interpret signs. There was good medicine, which brought good luck, and bad medicine, which attracted the opposite outcome! (*See* Beliefs.)

Medicine Man

A term for the shaman, who was a central figure in Indian life. The shaman (a word of Siberian origin) is supposed to hold the power to communicate with invisible forces that surround people. This skill was discovered early in the

Mandan

127

Sioux

lodges, fasts, and purging, and to many violent acts such as cutting and piercing with sharpened rocks and spines. One of the shaman's tasks was to take care of the sick. Indians thought that illnesses were a punishment, or an act of aggression by evil forces. So, taking care of the sick consisted of overpowering these demons. To achieve results, the shaman had a varied arsenal of objects and substances: magic stones, drums and rattles, herbs, pills, potions, ointments, needles, masks, feather fans, the skins of snakes and small mammals, bird heads, and the like. All of this was kept in a medicine chest,

Blackfoot

life of a child or adolescent (in rare cases, in girls).

Trained by one or many established shamans, the child then assumed his duties, which required him to lead a difficult way of life on the margins of the tribe. While the shaman was an important figure who had status and influence (he was considered to be the second most important figure in the tribe), his future wasn't one to be envied. He was often forbidden to marry, and lived alone, was feared, and was separated from other people. The shaman also subjected his body to various purification rites, such as sweat which was a gift from the shaman's initiator or from the society to which he belonged. Thus equipped, the shaman would attempt to chase the evil spirits out of the sick person's body, and for hours or days, he danced, prayed, and himself went through periods of trance and convulsions. Sometimes the shaman's work was successful, since confidence in the shaman's powers could act as a placebo and result in a cure. The shaman was thanked with gifts. The shaman was also supposed to interpret good and evil signs sent by the SPIRITS, and these sometimes affected serious decisions and the future of the tribe. This task was difficult and required more imagination than divination. Today no one can say whether the shamans were successful or not.

Menominee

• Their full name, *Menominiwoks*, means "wild rice people."
• Language: Algonquian.
• Their territory was located between Lake Michigan and Lake Superior in Wisconsin.

Harvesting wild rice

MEN

Menominees

• The Menominee were peaceful and sedentary and, despite their linguistic differences, were allies of the Winnebago in holding back their dangerous neighbors the Sauk and the Fox.
• The Menominee fished in the waters of the Great Lakes, gathered wild rice and harvested maple sugar. The Menominee women were known for their weaving talents. Using plant fibers or bison hair, they made bags and ribbons.
• The explorer Jean Nicolet encoun-

tered the Menominee in 1634. The Menominee participated in the PONTIAC revolt in 1763 and then avoided conflicts. However, a Menominee regiment was part of the northern troops in the Civil War.
• Descendants of the Menominee live today in the Great Lakes region. There were 3,800 Menominee in 1990, united under a tribal government.

Mesa Verde

A pueblo site discovered in 1888 in Southwestern Colorado. This was a true city that could house more than 7,000 people. It was occupied by the ANASAZI Indians from the sixth to the thirteenth century.

Mescalero
"Mescal People"
See Apaches.

Metacom

The second son of Massassoit, Metacom (also called Powetacom or, mockingly, "King Philip") became the chief of the WAMPANOAG after the death of his father and his older brother. For many years, Metacom was committed to keeping peace with the New England colonists. However, the intransigence of the English and the Indians' ongoing loss of their land led to conflict. In 1675–1676, "King Philip's War" ravaged both sides of the conflict. Indian villages were burned in response to raids and massacres against the whites. The conflict ended in Metacom's death and the bloody defeat of the allied tribes (Wampanoag and Narragansett).

Miami

• From the Algonquin-Chippewa word *Omaugeg*, meaning "people of the peninsula." The whites called the

Miami the Twight Wees, from their name *Twah twah*.
• Language: Algonquian.
• The Miami were semi-nomadic farmers and bison hunters. They originated in Wisconsin and then settled in northern Indiana and Illinois. The Miami tribes (Weas, Piankashaws, etc.) were more or less autonomous.
• After the departure of their French allies, the Miami went along with the efforts of Joseph Brant, Tecumseh, and LITTLE TURTLE (who was himself a Miami) in the resistance and fight against the despoilment of their lands.
• The descendants of the Miami live on a reservation in Oklahoma with the Peorias.
• There were 600 Miami in 1990.

Micmac

• From the word *Migmak*, meaning "ally."
• Language: Algonquian.
• The Micmac inhabited present-day New Brunswick and Prince Edward Island.
• They were semi-nomadic hunters and allies of the ABENAKI.
• They were undoubtedly seen by John Cabot who traveled along the coast in 1497. Jacques Cartier encountered them in the Saint Lawrence Gulf in 1534; the Micmacs approached him with furs as welcoming gifts, but he chased them away with cannon shots.
• Allied with the French, the Micmac delayed English settlement in Nova

Society" seemed so vast that in numerous tribes, everyone participated in ceremonies. To be a member of the SOCIETY, a dream or a vision was the beginning of the initiation process.

Miniconjou
"Those who plant by the water."
See Dakotas.

Missions
Following the first wave of Spanish, the "conquistadors," who were only concerned with wealth, the next arrivals were religious people whose mission was to evangelize and to convert the Indian peoples to the true faith. This task was primarily entrusted to the Franciscans and Dominicans, whose actions joined with the politics of Spain, which was concerned with preserving its influence on Mexico and California despite the competition from Russians and especially from the English on the Pacific coast.

Protected by the *presidios*, religious missions were first established in Texas, and later in California. They became tools for conquering and dominating the Indians. The Franciscans founded San Francisco in 1776 and established twenty-one missions in California, where Indian tribes were enslaved and subjected to *encomienda*, or forced labor. The Indians were poorly fed and poorly housed, and the reluctant among

Scotia and New Brunswick after helping to eliminate the Beothuk from Newfoundland in 1706.
• The Micmac still live in Nova Scotia. They numbered 8,645 in 1967.

Midewiwin
A movement that appeared in the Algonquin tribes of the Great Lakes in the seventeenth century. Its goal was to keep illnesses away, to prolong life, and to eliminate suffering. The powers attributed to this "Great Medicine

132

California Indians, before and after the arrival of missionaries

of many tributaries including the powerful Missouri River, the Mississippi symbolizes the history of the United States, and its nickname "Old Man River" evokes the nineteenth century, the conquest of the West and paddle boats.

Missouri

The Sioux called it "the muddy river." It was 2,341 miles (3,765 kilometers) long, beginning in the confluence of three rivers (the Jefferson, the Madison, and the Gallatin) in Tree Forks, Montana. It then gains the waters of many tributaries (the Yellowstone, Little Missouri, Cheyenne, White, Niobara, Dakota, Big Sioux, Platte, and Kansas) before joining the MISSISSIPPI upstream of Saint Louis. Here is how Meriwether LEWIS described his discovery of the waterfalls on the Missouri on June 13, 1805: "For 250 or 300 feet, the water falls in a smooth and regular mass . . . it offers the splendid spectacle of perfectly white foam . . . and over all of this the sun throws its most brilliant colors of the rainbow."

Missouri

• From the Algonquian "canoe owners." They called themselves *Niutachi*.

them were punished in the most cruel ways. According to the seriousness of the offense, they were put in handcuffs or leg irons, whipped, branded, and even mutilated or executed if they tried to escape. Violent revolts took place, and that resulted in a cycle of repression, hatred, and revenge.

Mississippi

From the Chippewa word *mici*, meaning "wide," and *zibi*, meaning "river."

The Mississippi is a 2,320-mile (3,694-kilometer) long river, which crosses the United States from north to south. Its source is in Lake Itasca in northern Minnesota. Strengthened by the waters

133

The Yellowstone River, before it meets the Missouri River

• They spoke a Siouan language, and belonged to the Chiwere group, along with the Iowa and the Oto.
• Settled on the southern bank of the Missouri River upstream of its confluence with the Mississippi.
• There were 1,000 Missouri in 1780, 80 in 1829, and 13 in 1910. In 1930 they were integrated into the Oto tribe.

Miwok

• Their name meant "people" in their language.
• Language: Penutian.
• The Miwok inhabited the region of Yosemite National Park (California), to the east of present-day San Francisco. They were hunters and farmers.

134

makisin (Chippewa). Like the shoes that we know by this name, Indian moccasins were made of animal skin and were light and flexible. They were made differently depending on the tribe. They were decorated depending on the imagination of the makers: with buttons, fabric or fur scraps, porcupine spines, etc. There were some types of moccasins for ceremonies.

Modoc

• From *Moatokni*, meaning "inhabi-tants of the south."
• Language: Shapwailutan.
• Lived in the northwest corner of the state of California (near Clear Lake and Goose Lake).
• There were 400 Modoc in 1780, 329 in 1937, and 133 in 1985.

Mogollon

Settled in the mountains of southern New Mexico, the Mogollon lived in a more rustic way than the HOHOKAM. Their half-buried dwellings were adapted to the extreme changes in temperature to which they were subjected. The Mogollon were hunters and gatherers, but also became skilled farmers, taking advantage of the proximity of water runoff from the mountains to grow corn, squash and beans.

The Mogollon were skilled potters and were also expert jewelers, using various materials in their work: turquoise from the region, copper from

• Subjected to the presence of the MIS-SIONS, they participated in many revolts. Some Miwok villages were ravaged by the Mexicans in 1843. The discovery of GOLD led miners in search of labor to carry out raids against certain tribes in order to bring back prisoners.
• There were approximately 11,000 Miwok in 1770, and only a few hundred survive today.

Mocassins

A name of Algonquian origin with many variations: *mockasin* (Powhatan), *mohkussin* (Massachusett), *mocussin* (Narragansset), *m'cusun* (Micmac),

Mexico, shells from the Pacific coast. In the thirteenth and fourteenth centuries, they migrated north and adopted the culture of their neighbors the Anasazi, the "cliff people." The Zunis are descendants of these Mogollon.

Mohave

• From *Hamakhava*, meaning "three mountains," in reference to the Needles Massif.
• Language: Hokan.

• Their territory was on the banks of the Colorado River, between the Needles range and the entrance to the Black Canyon.
• The Mohave were primarily farmers. Their warriors were known for their athletic qualities.
• After various bloody encounters with the Spanish beginning at the end of the sixteenth century, and then with the Americans, the Mohave's territory was made a reservation in 1865.
• Their population was estimated at 3,000 in 1680. They numbered 856 in 1937 and 2,650 in 1985.

Mohawk

See Iroquois.

Mohegan

• Their name meant "wolves," but they should not be confused with the Mahicans.
• Language: Algonquian.
• The Mohegan inhabited the valley of the Thornes River, which empties into the ocean in New London, Connecticut.
• Although the book *The Last of the Mohicans* is a work of fiction with no relationship to the Mohegan's history, it is likely that they, and not the Mahican, inspired this novel by James Fenimore COOPER (1826).

Monongahela

This battle, which took place in south-western Pennsylvania, near the pres-ent-day city of Pittsburgh, is one of the most famous battles in American history. On July 9, 1775, Monongahela marked the victory of the Indians and a small French force against the English and Virginians commanded by General Edward Braddock. It demonstrated the uselessness of battles fought in the compact "European" for-mation, and the superiority of Indian tactics such as speed, ambush, and individual combat.

Montagnais

See Naskapi.

Montcalm

Louis-Joseph (1712-1759)

Named Camp Marshal in 1756, Montcalm was sent to New France to defend the colony against the English. Despite a small number of troops, he heroically resisted the enemy until the Battle of Abraham, where he was mortally wounded. Four days after Montcalm's death, Quebec fell to the British.

Moose

This is the northern European elk; it is the largest cervid. *Alce Americana* can grow as large as a horse, and its antlers sometimes span more than 5 feet (1.5 meters). Moose are fond of swampy areas and leafy groves. In the summer, they often search alone for food: willow leaves and aquatic plants. In winter, moose travel in small herds and are content to find birch twigs and bark. For all of the Indians of the Great Forest, the moose was a prey enjoyed for its meat and hide. In the fall rutting period, Indians attracted the animals within the range of their arrows by using a call that simulated the mating call.

Mountain lion

This is the North American name for this carnivore (*Felis concolor*), which is better known by the name cougar, or puma in South America. The mountain

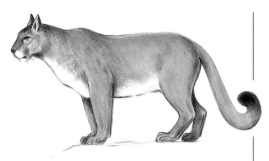

lion is the largest cat in North America. It prefers to hunt members of the deer family, but it does not disdain other prey: beavers, rodents, hares, birds, and even coyotes. Mountain lions are excellent climbers and are also impressive jumpers. Like so many other felines, the mountain lion is threatened with extinction today.

Mourning

The Indians were not obsessed with the afterlife. Since they held no concept of hell, the next world was similar to their world, and people in it were grouped by their manner of death: a warrior who was killed in combat apparently could not mingle on the eternal hunting grounds with a villager who died of old age. The Indians were primarily interested in the present, and the idea of death did not terrify them. On the contrary, they were preoccupied by ways of dying: being killed in battle seemed to them to be the most desirable way to go.

They were very afraid of ghosts, who, according to them, were the souls of dead braves who had suffocated, been tortured, or been mutilated, for example, scalped or disfigured warriors.

Old people who were unable to keep up with the tribe were simply abandoned, but the death of a warrior was cause for obvious expressions of sorrow: his wife hit herself, cut her hair, and inflicted terrible wounds on herself. Funerals were simple and quick; although tribal customs required burials, the dirt was simply leveled off with a few stones piled up to mark the spot. If cremation was the rule, the dead person was burned with his weapons and tools. Often, the deceased's favorite HORSE was sacrificed.

Other tribes abandoned the body in a cave, or in the fork of a tree. The Dakotas built a platform where the body would slowly decompose. The dead person's WEAPONS, tools, possessions, and dwelling were burned. For a long time afterward, the people who were close to the deceased would force themselves not to say his name, nor that of his TOTEM animal. Any trace of the dead person was thus erased: He was returned to the earth, the mother of all.

Music

Music was a part of all community events (ceremonies) and also of all events related to Indian life. Indian music was limited in its expression, partly because it was not written down, but was passed down from generation to generation, and partly because it was less important than nature and the capabilities of the instruments that were used: percussion (drums, bells, rattles) and melodic instruments (whistles, flutes, string instruments). The singing that accompanied the music could range from one to three octaves, and could include lyrics that related to the circumstances (celebrations, work, prayer, harvest, hunting, games, death) and also murmured sounds that set the rhythm for the chanting. Some songs "belonged" to clans or SOCIETIES, and only authorized people could perform them. This privilege could be bought. Errors in interpretation were punished! Most frequently, music and songs served as an accompaniment to dancers, so the percussion rhythm was often more important than the melody.

1 - Dakota flute
2 - Kiowa rattle
3 - Seneca rattle
4 - Dakota drum
5 - Navajo drum

Muskogean

See Languages, pg. 14.

Muskrat

Ondatra zizethiens is also known by the name ondatra. This large rodent is an excellent swimmer and lives on the banks of rivers, creeks, and ponds throughout North America. The muskrat's fur was very prized by trappers. In the absence of better game, the Indians sometimes settled for these small animals.

Mustang

See Horse.

N

Nahane

- "People of the setting sun."
- Language: Athabascan.
- The Nahane lived in northern British Columbia and in the Yukon.
- They were a nomadic people, living from hunting and gathering. The Nahane's way of life was similar to that of their neighbors.
- There were 2,000 Nahane in British Columbia and 800 in the Yukon in 1670. Today, there are approximately 1,000.

Nanticoke

- From *Nentego* (a variant of *Unechtgo* or *Unalachtigo*), "people of the tide-water."
- Language: Algonquian.
- The Nanticoke lived along the coast of Maryland and in southern Delaware. They were faithful allies of the Iroquois of the League of Five Nations.
- There were 1,600 Nanticoke in 1600 and 700 in 1915.

Narragansett

- "People of the small point."
- Language: Algonquian.
- Settled on the west side of Narragansett Bay in Rhode Island.
- The Narragansett were led jointly by two SACHEMS, ideally a man and his nephew.
- They were semi-nomadic and grew corn and beans. They were good hunters, and fished for shellfish and seafood. Narragansett women were accomplished artisans, which allowed the Narragansett to prosper, notably because of the trade in WAMPUM.
- The Narragansett were allies of the English during the PEQUOT war, and

they were hard-hit by epidemics in the seventeenth century.
• They numbered 4,000 in 1600, and 2,500 currently live in Rhode Island.

Narvaez
Panfilo (1470-1529)

Narvaez was a Spanish conquistador who had the reputation of being brutal and roguish. After conquering Cuba, he led an expedition to take possession of Florida (1528). Harassed by the TIMUCUA, his troops had to set off in a hurry on five rafts. They ran aground at Galveston Island. Four people survived, including NUNEZ CABEZA DE VACA.

Naskapi

• The Naskapi and the MONTAGNAIS are considered to be one and the same people. The Montagnais lived in southern Labrador between the Saint Lawrence estuary and James Bay, and the Naskapi settled in central Labrador. The Montagnais owe their name to the French, to the French (from the French *montagne*, meaning "mountain") due to the topography of their region. They called themselves *Ne-Enoilno*, "perfect people." The Naskapi were so called by the Montagnais, Naskapi being a term of reproach meaning rustic, rough

or hard. The Naskapi called themselves *Na-Nenot*, "the true people."
• Language: Algonquian.
• The Montagnais were hunters and fishermen. The Naskapi hunted CARIBOU and small game, and also fished for trout. The women of the tribe made smoked meat and fish.
• The Micmac and especially the IROQUOIS were enemies of the Montagnais. The Naskapi's enemies were the INUIT, who lived more to the north. The Montagnais were largely christianized and were faithful partners of the French in trade and in war. They were threatened

Naskapi

with extinction due to the scarcity of fur-bearing animals, famine, war and epidemics.
• 7,000 Montagnais and a few hundred Naskapi live in Quebec.

Natchez

• The etymology of their name is uncertain. It may mean "warriors of the great cliff."
• Language: Muskogean.
• The Natchez lived along the most southern part of the Mississippi.
• In addition to their skills as weavers, the Natchez were known for their

theocratic tribal organization, centered around an authoritarian monarch, the Great Sun. A sacred fire burned perpetually under their altars. Social relations were subject to a strict hierarchy.
• The Natchez were the oldest and largest tribe in the region. They were practically eliminated in 1729–1730 during their revolt against the French. The survivors dispersed, and some were sent as slaves to Saint-Domingue (present-day Haiti).
• The Natchez population was estimated at 4,500 in 1650; today they have disappeared.

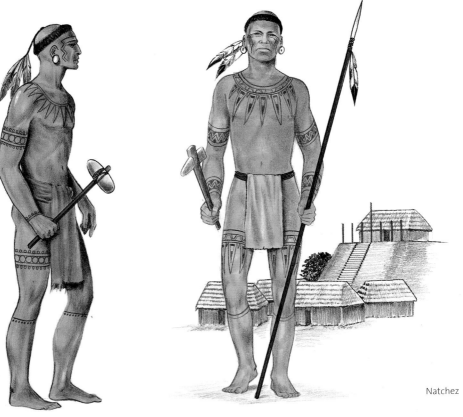

Natchez

Natchitoches

See Caddos.

Navajo

- Language: Athabascan.
- The Navajo settled in northwestern New Mexico and northeastern Arizona. Their traditional dwelling, the HOGAN, was made of wood and earth.
- More sedentary than the other Athabascans, the Navajo were farmers (corn and fruit) and became skilled at raising sheep. The Navajo demonstrated uncommon skill in all artistic areas: BASKET WEAVING, weaving, and metal working (splendid silver jewelry).

- From *Navahuu* or *Nauajo,* "large fields," which became Navajo or Navaho. The Navajo called themselves *Dineh,* "the people."

• The Navajo religious universe is composed of a visible world, the one in which they live, surrounded by animals and plants, and an invisible world. The invisible world is the kingdom of the gods, SPIRITS, and ancestors. Offerings, ceremonial dances, incantations, prayers and sand paintings were part of the complex rituals intended for these gods.

• Originally from the north like their cousins the Apache, the Navajo were influenced by the customs of the Pueblos, whose revolt they took part in in 1680. The Navajo were unaffected by the work of missionaries and continued to fight against the Spanish. Two treaties (in 1846 and 1849) did not end their actions. In 1863 Colonel Kit CARSON, responsible for making the Indians see reason, burned their fields, massacred their livestock and imprisoned a large part of the tribe, 300 miles (500 kilometers) from their home. The Navajo were freed in 1867 and were able to go back to their lands; peace with their neighbors was finally established.

• The Navajo are spread over many reservations in Arizona, New Mexico and Utah. Through their skills and initiative, they have enriched their community by earning money from sheep raising, oil drilling rights for wells on their lands, and tourism-related activities.

• Estimated at 8,000 in 1680, today the Navajo probably number more than 220,000. Their 40,000 square mile (65,000 square kilometer) territory is by far the largest granted to an Indian people.

Navajo weaving

Neutral

• Name given by the French to denote their neutrality in the war between the Iroquois and the Huron.

• Language: Iroquoian.

• Settled on the banks of Lake Erie.

• There were 10,000 Neutrals in 1600. They were exterminated by the Iroquois in 1650.

Nez Perce

- The name, meaning "pierced nose" in French, was given to this group of Indians because some members wore shell ornaments in their noses. The Nez Perce called themselves *Numiipu*, "The People."
- Language: Sahaptian.
- They inhabited a large part of Idaho and northeastern Oregon (in the Snake and Clearwater River valleys).
- The Nez Perce hunted BISON, and were heavily involved in raising APPALOOSA horses.
- The Nez Perce were very peaceful; however, they opposed the activities of trappers between 1830 and 1840. They gave away a large part of their territory in the Walla Walla treaty of 1855, but their reservation was invaded by gold seekers in 1860. Following the treaty of 1863, they kept only the Lapwai reservation. In 1877 the decision to open the Wallowa Valley provoked the Nez Perce revolt, led by CHIEF JOSEPH. Their tragic journey came to an end in 1878.
- The Nez Perce population was estimated at 4,000 in 1780. In 1995, 3,300 Nez Perce were counted on the Lapwai reservation in Oregon.

Nisqually

- The meaning of their name is unknown.
- Language: Salishan.
- Lived along the lower part of the Nusqually River in Washington state.
- They numbered 3,600 in 1780 and 62 in 1937. There are probably 1,700 on the reservation in Washington, but this number undoubtedly includes other Salish.

Nez Perce

Nootka

- They were visited early on by Juan de Fuca (1592) and then by Perez (1774), Cook (1778), and Vancouver (1792). The founding of Victoria, British Columbia (1843) marked the end of their cultural independence. The Nootka were converted to Catholicism.
- There were 6,000 Nootka in 1780 and 3,200 in 1967, spread throughout the province of British Columbia, Canada.

- The origin of their name is unknown.
- Language: Wakashan (first division with the Makah).
- Occupied the west coast of Vancouver Island. Their large rectangular houses, made of cedar wood, were oriented facing the sea.
- The Nootka were great hunters of marine mammals such as WHALES, SEALS, and dolphins. Along with the Makah, they were the only Indians to travel on the high seas in pursuit of cetaceans.

Nuñez Cabeza de Vaca
Alvaro (1490-1560)

He was one of the survivors of the NARVAEZ expedition. Unlike Narvaez, he was a loyal and good man; after the expedition's shipwreck near Galveston, Texas, he was taken prisoner by the Indians and escaped with three other survivors. He wandered through northern Texas, took care of the Indians, and was considered by them to be a MEDICINE MAN. Welcomed by the Pimas, he was a witness to the atrocities committed during the Spanish incursions. Also, upon his return to Mexico, he attempted to change the conquerors' mindset regarding the indigenous populations. The story of his extraordinary journey, leading one to believe that fabulous riches existed in the north, foreshadowed the expeditions of DE SOTO and CORONADO.

O

Oglala

"They scatter their own."
A division of the Lakota. (*See* Dakota.)

Ohio

An abbreviation of *Ohioniio*, "beautiful river." The Ohio River is a western tributary of the Mississippi. The Ohio Valley was a major route of penetration for the colonists attracted by the fertile land.

Ojibwa

• Also called Chippewa. The Ojibwa called themselves *An-ish-in-aub-ag*, "spontaneous people." The Cree called them "those who speak the same language," to the Hurons they were "the waterfall people," and the French called them the Saulteaux, an allusion to the waterfalls in Sault-Sainte-Marie.
• Language: Algonquian.
• Like the Cree, the Ojibwa were divided into plains tribes and forest tribes; the forest tribes occupied the northern bank of Lake Superior.
• The Ojibwa were semi-nomadic hunters and gathered wild rice along Lake Superior. They were also renowned as fishermen and canoe

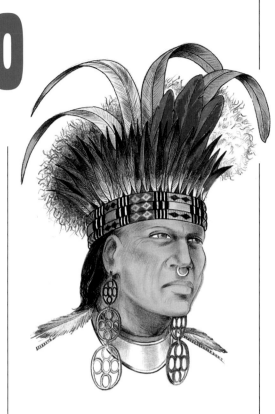

builders. Their birch bark shelters were made by the Ojibwa women.
They actively participated in fur trading. They were allied with the Ottawa and the Potawatomi, particularly against the Fox. They fought alongside the English against the American insurgents and participated in the revolts of LITTLE TURTLE (1790) and TECUMSEH (1812).
• Their population was estimated at 30,000 individuals in 1905. The Ojibwa population lives around the U.S.–Canada border, about half on reservations. Today, the population probably exceeds 105,000 persons.

147

Okeepa

For the MANDAN, this was an annual ceremony devoted to the return of the BISON, similar to the Sun Dance done by the plains tribes. It began with the "male bison" dance (not to be confused with the bison dance), symbolic of the species' reproduction and migration, which was essential to the life of the tribe. The ceremony continued with an initiation ritual for the young men. This involved terrifying tests: wooden pegs were inserted under the muscles of the back and chest, and were used

to hang the young warriors from the roof of the "medicine hut." Using other pegs and small dowels placed in the arms and legs, shields and bison skulls were hung from the men's bodies in order to put more weight on them. Suspended in this way, the tortured men dangled for 15–20 minutes from a tree trunk installed in the center of the hut. The ceremony ended with a race on the village square, where the young warriors, still bleeding, were dragged over the ground with the shield and the bison skull still attached to their limbs. George CATLIN attended this ceremony and wrote a detailed description of it.

Oklahoma

From a Choctaw word meaning "man with red skin." This diverse territory was initially reserved for the FIVE CIVILIZED TRIBES (Cherokee, Choctaw, Chickasaw, Creek, and Seminole), and they were deported to it between 1830 and 1833 along the TRAIL OF TEARS, under harsh conditions that resulted in many deaths along the way. It was even planned to create an Indian state that could some day join the Union. Forgetting these good intentions, on April 22, 1889, the authorities allowed thousands of people to invade the Indians' territory and to seize land for themselves. In a few hours, a million hectares was distributed to the colonists. Oklahoma became a state in the Union in 1907.

Omaha

- "Those who march against the wind." They formed one of the Dhegiha tribes (along with the Ponca, Osage, and Kansas).
- Language: Siouan.
- Lived in northeastern Nebraska, on the western bank of the Missouri.
- Their villages were made of shelters covered with earth or bark. But when they hunted BISON, they used TIPIS like the other prairie tribes.
- The Omaha were in conflict with the Dakota, but had good relations with the whites. They sold all their land in 1854, with the exception of a parcel that became their reservation. In 1865 a piece of land allocated to the Winnebago was removed from their reservation.
- There were 2,800 Omaha in 1780 and 1,300 in 1970.

Oneida

See Iroquois.

Onondaga

See Iroquois.

Orca

A cetacean mammal, the orca (*Orcinus orca*) is also called a killer whale, or whale killer. It can reach 30 feet (9 meters) in length, and it has a voracious appetite: fish, squid, turtles, and water birds are its usual prey. It is frequently represented on the TOTEMS of the Indians of the northern Pacific coast.

Oregon Trail

In 1846 the English gave the Americans possession of a vast region then called Oregon; it included the present-day states of Oregon, Idaho, and Washington. The Oregon Trail made it possible to link the east with Vancouver. It was used by colonists, trappers, gold seekers, and adventurers. Crossing the territories of the Dakota, the Cheyenne, the Ponca, and the Plateau Indians (Cayuse, Nez Perce, and Yakima), the consequences of its existence are easy to imagine!

Osage

• A corruption of their name, *Wazhazhe*, by French traders.
• Language: Siouan.
• Settled in the area of southern Missouri and northern Arkansas.
• The Osage are the largest Dhegiha tribe. Their organization is identical to that of other tribes in the group: lineage is through the father, marriage between members of the same clan is prohibited, clans are specialized in their activity to serve the community. The tribe was separated into two halves: the war half and the peace half.
• Jacques MARQUETTE encountered them in 1673. They were allied with the French to defeat the Fox in 1714. They were then noted for their intense warring

activity, their name becoming synonymous with "enemy" to other Indians. In 1802, French traders persuaded them to travel up the Arkansas River and settle in what would become Oklahoma. They were successively subjected to the arrival of tribes that were driven out of the eastern part of the continent and to the invasion of white colonists.

- They then settled on a reservation in Kansas, and settled permanently in Oklahoma in 1870.
- There were 6,200 Osage in 1780 and 9,500 in 1995.

Osceola
(1803-1838)

A SEMINOLE chief who, from his refuge in the swamps of Florida, fought against the Americans in the second Seminole war (1835–1838). Osceola wanted to negotiate with General Jessup and went to Fort Moultrie, North Carolina, with a white flag. Osceola was tricked and imprisoned. Shortly before dying of malaria, he received a visit in his cell from George CATLIN, who was scandalized by Osceola's detention.

Oto

- From *Wat'ota*, translated as "libertine." Their name could more likely mean "fickle." Along with the Iowa and the Missouri, they are one of the three tribes in the Chiwere Sioux division.
- Language: Siouan.
- Settled in Nebraska, on the lower portion of the Platte River.

- The Oto were semi-nomadic farmers and hunters.
- In their migration toward the west, the Oto were separated first from the Iowa and then from the Missouri. They were visited by Cavelier de La Salle in 1680 and gave up their land in 1854. When their reservation on the Big Blue River was sold in 1881, they left for Oklahoma, where they shared reservations with the Ponca, Pawnee, and Missouri.
- With a population of 900 in 1780, they numbered 1,300 in 1985.

151

Ottawa

• From the Algonquian *adawe*, meaning "trade."
• Language: Algonquian.
• Lived on the banks of Georgian Bay and Manitoulin Island, on the northern end of Lake Huron.
• They participated in the traditional activities of the Great Lakes Algonquin; sedentary in the summer in small villages surrounded by corn fields, semi-nomadic in the winter along rivers and streams and in pursuit of game.
• Pushed back by the Iroquois to the north of Lake Michigan, they were unconditional allies of the French. After the Treaty of Paris (1763), their chief, PONTIAC, refused English hegemony and continued the battle.

• The Ottawa were part of Joseph BRANT's federation of Indian nations, who were hostile to American expansion. But they transferred their lands to the federal government through successive treaties (1785, 1789, 1795, and 1836).
• There is an Ottawa reservation in Oklahoma, and numerous Ottawa live in Michigan, Ontario, and on their ancestral island, Manitoulin.

Otter

The sea otter (*Enhydra lutris*) can swim very quickly while staying under water for 4 or 5 minutes. Otters feed on shellfish, crabs, sea urchins, and small fish. They build nests out of algae for sleeping and take refuge on land in case of danger (approaching orcas or sharks, storms, etc.). The tribes of the Northwest excelled in capturing otters and tanning otter skins, which they traded with the whites.

P

Paintings

The first Europeans who landed on the shores of the New World were impressed by the body paintings on the people they would call Indians. Initially, these paintings undoubtedly had a role in protecting against sun, wind and insects, but with time, they served to indicate the person's rank or war prowess and to confer protective powers. They could also vary according to the circumstances (wars, ceremonies, etc.). The warriors of the Plains saw their body paintings as a way of making an impression on their adversaries, and their HORSES were often decorated as well, with paintings that boasted about the mount as well as the rider. Each person wore the insignia of his clan, frequently a protective animal such as the WOLF or fox. In fact, the paintings were only a mix of a fatty base with vegetable, animal, or mineral-based pigments. For example, wild sunflower was used for yellow, different berries for red, hickory nuts for black, duck excrement for blue, red dirt for ocher yellow, copper powder for charcoal, and so on.

Paiute

- Their name might mean "the true Utes."
- Language: Shoshonean.
- The northern branch of the Paiutes lived in northern Nevada and southwestern Oregon; the southern branch lived in southern Nevada and southeastern Utah.
- Organized in small autonomous bands in the eighteenth century, they lived in a comparable situation to the stone age. They hunted deer and rabbits, and ate meat and crushed bones. They evolved thanks to mastering the farming of

153

Facial Paint

Blackfoot

Iowa

Pawnee

Téton

154

- Settled on the banks of the Palouse River (Washington and Idaho).
- Allies of the NEZ PERCE, the Palus were bison hunters.
- From 1848 to 1858, they, along with other tribes, resisted pressure from whites. They were the last to fight, and even though they were included in the treaty of 1855, they refused to live on a RESERVATION.
- There were 1,600 Palus in 1805, and 82 were counted in 1910.

certain crops such as corn, pumpkins, beans, and sunflowers.
- When gold prospectors and colonists descended on the route to the west after 1850, it was the Mormons who armed the Indians in an effort to avoid this invasion. The northern Paiute were allocated RESERVATIONS beginning in 1865, and the southern Paiute were granted reservations some decades later. They participated in the revolt of the Bannocks in 1878 and a Paiute, WOWOKA, preached the worship of the GHOST DANCE in 1890.
- There were 11,000 Paiute in 1995 on reservations in Nevada (Duck Valley, Pyramid Lake, Walker River) and on ranches in California.

Palous

- Etymology and meaning unknown.
- Language: Shahaptian/Penutian.

Papago

• "Bean people." They called them-selves *Tono-oohtan*, meaning "people of the desert." They are distant descen-dants of the Hohokam.
• Language: Uto-Aztecan.
• They lived to the south and southwest of the present-day city of Tucson, Ari-zona, and beyond the Mexican border.
• The Papagos were a semi-sedentary tribe, and moved depending on the rare rainfall in the region. They grew corn and cotton.
• Allies of the PIMA, the Papago were discovered by Father Eusebio Kino in 1694.
• There were 6,000 Papago in 1700, 4,300 in 1937 and 8,300 in 1995.

Papoose

This Algonquian word refers to small CHILDREN. There were different forms specific to different tribes: *pappouse, peiss, papeisse, papeississu*. This word was undoubtedly inspired by the first sounds that a young child made. It is interesting to associate it with the Latin word *pupus*, meaning "child." In most tribes, the papoose spends its first months in a baby carrier, a sort of cradle attached to a piece of wood and placed on the mother's back, on a tree trunk or on the flank of a horse. By age 5, boys and girls knew how to swim. After that, they learned different skills depending on their sex; boys were taught the art of hunting, fishing, camouflaging them-selves, using a bow and arrow, and rid-

Crow cradle

ing HORSES; girls discovered the secrets of gathering food, preparing meals, or tanning animal skins.

Parfleche

A bag made of animal hide which was used by the Plains Indians. Along with BASKET WEAVING, the parfleche offered nomadic peoples the advantage of being less fragile than POTTERY. The Indians used parfleches to carry various objects and personal clothing as well as to store certain food reserves such as PEMMICAN.

Passamaquoddy

• "Those who fish for pollock" (pollock is a fish similar to the cod; it inhabits the waters along the Atlantic coast).
• Language: Algonquian.
• Inhabited the lower part of the St. Croix River between Maine and New Brunswick.
• There was a stable population of 400 individuals until 1930; it grew to 1,070 by 1985.

Paul III
(1468-1549)

Became Pope in 1534. Since the beginning of the sixteenth century, religious men had encouraged Rome to denounce the brutal methods that the Spanish warriors used against the Indians. In 1511 the Dominican Antonio de Montesinos delivered a homily entitled *Ego vox clamantis in deserto*, protesting against the treatment imposed on the Indians. In 1515, LAS CASAS interceded with Charles V and Philip II. In 1532 eight Franciscans sent a plea to the "Indies Council" in Madrid, and a Dominican, Domingo de Betanzos, inspired Paul III to write *Sublimus Deus* on June 2, 1537. "The Indians and all the other peoples who, in the future, might be discovered, even in a time when they will still be outside of the Christian faith, must not be deprived of their liberty and of the ownership of their possessions. They must fully enjoy these, and we must never reduce them to servitude. Any action to the contrary, in any way in which it is performed, is invalid, null, without force or value."

Pawnee

• From *Paariki*, meaning "horned," a reference to their hair style, or from *Parisu*, "hunter." They called themselves *Chakiksichahiks*, which means "men of men."

157

PAW

- Language: Caddoan.
- Lived along the lower part of the Platte River in Nebraska.
- Divided into four bands, the Pawnee were seminomadic, living in earth-covered shelters. Like the MANDAN, they combined corn farming and bison hunting. They observed complex religious rituals where the natural elements (wind, thunder, stars, rain) were

messages sent by Tirawahat, the supreme force. A series of ceremonies marked the growth of the corn and sometimes involved human sacrifice (generally of a Comanche captive). The Pawnee practiced BASKET WEAVING, POTTERY, and weaving.
- The Pawnee came from the south and occupied the Plains before the arrival of the Sioux. Coronado encountered them in 1541. At the beginning of the eighteenth century, the Pawnee were allied with the French for trade and to counter the pressure from the Spanish. They succumbed in their battles against the DAKOTA. They supplied scouts to the

158

U.S. armies, which fomented the hatred of the Sioux tribes. They Pawnee gave up their land through treaties and settled in Oklahoma.
• There were approximately 10,000 Pawnee in 1780 and 2,000 in 1990.

Pemmican

BISON meat dried in the sun was ground into powder and mixed with fat and wild berries; the resulting mixture was then stored in animal skin pouches or in segments of intestine. This was the Indian version of sausage! Easy to store and rich in protein, pemmican was an ideal insurance against famine. The hunters and warriors of the Plains and the Subarctic brought pemmican with them when they left their villages for many weeks.

Penn
William
(1644-1718)

Associated with Quaker philosophy, this Englishman organized the settlement of many thousands of emigrants fleeing Europe and religious persecution. The Quakers opted for a territory given as a concession by the King of England, which then became Pennsylvania (Penn's own last name followed by the Latin word *sylvania*, meaning "forest").

Penn founded the city of Philadelphia and succeeded in establishing relationships of friendship and trust with the Indians. Unlike other colonists, the Quakers, who were deeply egalitarian, recognized the indigenous peoples' right to land ownership.

Pennacook
• Meaning "at the bottom of the hill."
• Language: Algonquian.
• Their territory included parts of New Hampshire, Maine, and Massachusetts around the present-day city of Boston.
• The Pennacook abandoned their territory at the end of the seventeenth century to join the ABENAKI in northern Maine.
• There were 2,000 Pennacook in 1600 and 280 in 1924.

Penobscot
• Meaning "the place where there are rocks."
• Language: Algonquian.
• The Penobscot lived in the delta of the Penobscot River in Maine.
• They were visited by CHAMPLAIN in 1604 and were allied with the French against the English until 1749 when the conflict ended.
• There were 1,106 Penobscot in 1985 on their reservation.

Penutian
See Languages, pg. 15.

Peoria

See Illinois.

Pequot

- Meaning "destroyers."
- Language: Algonquian.
- The Pequot inhabited the southeastern coast of the present-day state of Connecticut.
- After fairly cordial contacts, the Pequots felt threatened by the Dutch and the English. Under the direction

of Chief Sassacus, they tried to rally their neighbors and rose up against the white invaders (1637). The repression was so brutal that old tribal rivalries returned. In support of the English, the Mohegans and the Narragansetts

caused the defeat of the insurgents, who were mercilessly massacred. The few survivors of the "Pequot War" were sold as slaves.
- There were 2,200 Pequots in 1600, 140 in 1762, and 200 in 1990.

Permafrost

Permafrost is a crust of frozen soil from 100 to 1,000 feet (30 to 300 meters) thick, which covers the Subarctic TUNDRA. In the spring, the sun melts the snow and ice to a depth of 66 to 82 feet (20 to 25 meters), which allows lichens and plants to grow. These serve as food for mammals and attract the flights of migrating birds. This marks the beginning of a short hunting period, but one that is of the utmost importance for the peoples of the region.

Peyote

A cactus that is native to Mexico. Its hallucinogenic properties led to a worship of the plant, which spread throughout the Great Plains beginning in 1840. The Kiowa and Comanche were the primary users of peyote

Piankashaw

See Miami.

Pictograms

The Indians did not write but used pictograms, or symbolic drawings, to preserve and magnify the memory of the important events in their lives. Pictograms were done on stretched animal skins or on bark, and they also made it possible to establish chronology by counting the number of winters.

Pima

- They called themselves *Aa-tam*, "water people."
- Language: Piman, a subdivision of Uto-Aztecan.
- The Pima inhabited the valleys of the Gila River and its tributary, the Salt River, near the present-day city of Phoenix.
- Beginning at the end of the seventeenth century, the Spanish made the Pima their allies by capitalizing on their hostility toward the Apache. Using the same logic, the Americans armed the Pima to contain the Apache revolts.
- There were 4,000 Pima in 1680, 5,170 in 1937, and 14,000 in 1990.

Cherokee

Iroquois

Great Plains

Pipes

Aside from the CALUMET, which was used for official or sacred matters, the Indians, who were great lovers of TOBACCO, used pipes of different shapes depending on the region. The pipes were made of POTTERY, wood, bone, metal, catlinite or stone, and sometimes included two of these materials. TOMA-HAWKS, which combined the functions of a pipe and an ax, were made by the Europeans.

Plains Cree

- Language: Algonquian.
- Allies of the Assiniboines against their common enemies the Siksikas and the Dakotas. Some of them participated, along with their chiefs Poundmaker and Big Bear and the Assiniboines, in the Burned Forest revolt (1885), which had established a provisional government in Saskatchewan.

161

• The Plains Cree population was estimated at approximately 4,000 in the middle of the nineteenth century; their descendants joined the Forest Cree on their reservation or integrated with other tribes.

Plateau

See The Indian Lands, p. 11.

Pocahontas

(circa 1595-1617)

This is a variation of her actual name, Matohata. Pocahontas was the daughter of king POWHATAN, and she defended Captain John SMITH, who was sentenced to death by her father. Despite these good omens, the relationships between colonists and Indians deteriorated, and Pocahontas (meaning "little mischievous one") was taken prisoner by the English, who forced Powhatan to pay a ransom for her. Once freed, Pocahontas married a prosperous tobacco planter named John Rolfe, as a peace pledge. She was soon baptized under the name Rebecca and went to England in 1616 to be introduced to the royal family. The young Indian died of tuberculosis before seeing her native country again.

Pomo

• Their name means "people" in their language. Pomo was also a suffix associated with village names (such as Ballokaipomo, Yokayapomo, etc.).
  • Language: Hokan.
  • The Pomo lived in the coastal region of California, north of San Francisco.
  • They lived from gathering (berries and acorns were the basis of their diet), hunting small game, and fishing. They were known for their simplicity, but they also demonstrated great skill at carving on shells and drift objects. The Pomo women practiced BASKET WEAVING that was the most elaborate in California, using varied techniques and materials.
• The Pomo largely escaped the influence of the Franciscan MISSIONS, but

they had to fight against the Mexicans and then against GOLD seekers.

• Their population was estimated at 8,000 in 1770 and about 1,000 in 1985.

Ponca

• The meaning of their name is unknown.
• Language: Siouan.
• The Ponca lived at the confluence of the Niobrara and Missouri Rivers in Nebraska.
• They came from the OMAHA tribe and followed the same way of life as all of the Dhegiha Sioux.

• They were conquered by their "enemy brothers" the DAKOTA and deported to Oklahoma in 1877. Led by chief Standing Bear, a minority refused to leave their territory, of which a part became a reservation in 1889. Until his death in 1908, Standing Bear fought for the recognition of his people's rights.
• The Ponca population was estimated at 800 in 1780. There were 400 Ponca in Nebraska in 1944 and 2,200 in Oklahoma in 1985.

Ponce de León
Juan (1460-1521)

A companion of Christopher Columbus, this Spanish nobleman was traveling north from Cuba, and on May 27, 1513, landed at a place he named Florida, "the land of flowers." The TIMUCUA gave the visitors a cordial welcome, but then a small incident erupted into a battle. Ponce de León raised anchor and came back 8 years later: The Indians were waiting for the Spanish and Ponce de León was injured. He died upon his return to Cuba. Thus, this first exploration of the continent began on a worrisome note.

Pontiac
(circa 1720-1769)

An OTTAWA chief, "Pontiac" is a variation of his actual name, Obwandiyag.

Pontiac was opposed to English expansion and preferred to support the goals of the French. He devised an ambitious plan for mobilizing an alliance of all of the southern Great Lakes tribes (Huron, Ojibwa, Potawatomi). The "Pontiac Revolt" was launched in 1763 and inflamed the region, but it ended in failure when the French withdrew from the plan. Defeated by Detroit, Pontiac resigned himself to signing a peace treaty in 1765. Four years later, he died after being assassinated by an Illinois Indian who had been bribed by the English.

Porcupine

The American porcupine (*Erethizon dorsatum*) is larger than its European cousin. The porcupine is nocturnal, sleeping during the day in a burrow or a hollow tree. It is not an aggressive animal and prefers to retreat rather than fight. When porcupines are forced to fight, they protect themselves with their spines and try to hit their opponent with their tail. A porcupine's spines can then detach and get stuck in the enemy's skin, where they are firmly embedded. These spines were used as decorations for Indian clothing and moccasins.

Potawatomi

- Literally means "people of the place of fire." They were known as the nation of fire.

- Language: Algonquian.
- The Potawatomi occupied the western shore of Lake Michigan.
- The Potawatomi were semi-nomadic hunters and fishermen. They fished at night by installing lights on the prows of their boats.
- Allied with the French against the English, the Potawatomi were active participants in the unsuccessful PONTIAC revolt in 1763. The Potawatomi settled

in Indiana and opposed American colonization. They were expelled in 1846 and settled in Kansas where they had conflicts with the Pawnee.

• Their descendants live on reservations in Oklahoma and Kansas. Some of them have returned to the area south of the Great Lakes. There were 16,700 Potawatomi in 1990.

Potlatch

A word of Chinook origin. Potlatch was part of a custom of the Indians of the northwest coast and accompanied various celebrations such as marriages, births, funerals and earning titles. For the person receiving it, potlatch consisted of supplying a large amount of food and gifts to the guests. This redistribution of goods that had been acquired through work (jewelry, furs, blankets, canoes, etc.) or war conquests (weapons, food, prisoners) was the chance for a person to show his wealth, nobility, and generosity. It could also challenge a rival to do the same, if the rival wanted to prove his prestige and not lose face. Potlatch is a social ritual that reinforces the tribe's cohesiveness. Because of some excesses such as indebtedness, which became more and more common, the Canadian government forbade potlatch between 1884 and 1951.

Pottery

Most tribes were talented basket weavers, but only the people of the

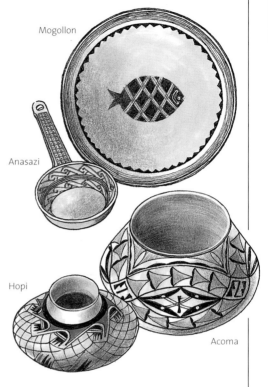

Mogollon

Anasazi

Hopi

Acoma

southwest engaged in pottery. They undoubtedly inherited this skill from pre-Columbian cultures (Anasazi, Hohkam, Mogollon, etc.) who left many remains behind. The ZUNI, the HOPI, and certain PUEBLO Indians still continue this active tradition.

Power

Although there were numerous authoritarian regimes in Europe, they were the exception for the North American Indians, undoubtedly because the Indian character did not tolerate the arbitrary nature of absolute power.

The Indians were democratic, but in their own way, which wasn't the worst way. Every entity, family, clan, brotherhood, and half-tribe had a chief, who was most often co-opted and chosen for his wisdom, experience, and good sense. Chiefs largely took on the role of guiding and counseling rather than directing. Maybe because they feared the personalization of power, the Indians considered both chiefs of each half-tribe to be equals, but assigned different tasks to them. Thus, for numerous Indian peoples, there was a "civil" chief and a "military" chief, one who led the tribe in times of peace, the other in times of war. In some tribes, such as the Osage, the civil chief was vegetarian, and the military chief ate meat. Some other power-sharing arrangements were more poetic: The Pueblo had summer and winter governments, the Winnebago had a sky half and an earth half. Decisions were made jointly by a counsel that included all the chiefs of the tribe. The elders, who were supposed to be wiser, assisted the chiefs in making legal decisions. Together, they decided what punishments to apply for all possible crimes: murder, theft, adultery, assault, insults, and more. The penalties were generally strict and swift. Murder was punished by the death of the guilty person, and, if that person had escaped, a male from his family was forced to take his place. In certain tribes, adultery was punished by mutilation of the ears, lips, or nose and sometimes

even by death. Other crimes resulted in fines or corporal punishment: the guilty person was whipped, or had his skin marked with spines or pointed bones.

Powhatan

• This was a confederation of tribes joined under the authority of Wahunsonacock (1550–1618), the chief of the Potomacs (the Pamukey, Pocomoke, Nansemond, Wicomi, and Mattaponi). The whites called him Powhatan (he was Pocahontas's father) and this name soon came to include all of the Indians of this confederation.

Here:

- Language: Algonquian.
- The Powhatan settled on the coast of Virginia and Maryland.
- They were farmers (corn, pumpkins, beans) and also hunted and fished.
- They were the first to suffer the white invasion. Between 1607, when Jamestown was founded, and 1675, there was a continuous string of massacres, punishment expeditions, vengeances, and truces. In some 60 years, the Powhatan tribes were reduced to a few sparse bands.

Powwow

This word, of Algonquian origin, had many forms (*powow, pawaw, pauwau*), and meant "he practices divination," or more simply "he dreams." These words focus on the sense of gathering, counsel, or celebration, but it might also mean MEDICINE MAN, signifying the shaman's work with a patient or the dance preceding a celebration. For the nomadic Plains people, the powwow served an essential function of social cohesion. It allowed scattered tribes to get together at least once a year, to trade news and to cement alliances. A powwow that was worthy of the name lasted many days and included singing, dancing, feasting, and games.

Pronghorn antelope

The pronghorn antelope is an abundant game animal but is also difficult to hunt. It was a primary food source for the western Indians. The pronghorn is the fastest animal in the New World, and can attain speeds of over 43 miles (70 kilometers) per hour, and leap more than 19 feet (6 meters).

Pueblo Bonito

This was the site of an Anasazi village in Chaco Canyon, New Mexico. Construction began in about A.D.1000; the village was spread out on terraces in a half-circle and included 600 rooms that could house more than 1,000 people.

Pueblos

- The Spanish used this word, meaning "city" or "village" in their language for the Indians who lived in dwellings made of ADOBE (bricks of earth dried in the sun). These peoples, using different

167

languages, lived peacefully together farming their lands, as they had done for centuries.

• The arrival in 1540 of Francisco Vasquez de CORONADO sounded the death knell for their tranquility and led to pillage and killings. Bit by bit, missionaries and Spanish soldiers moved in, some to convert the Indians and some to enslave them. The Pueblo Indians revolted against these invaders in 1680, but at the end of the seventeenth century, the Spanish returned. The majority of the Pueblo tribes lived in New Mexico (Jemez, Keresan Pueblo, Piro Pueblo, Tewa Pueblo, Tiwa Pueblo, Zuni) and others in Arizona (Hopi).

• There were 53,000 Pueblo in 1990.

Puyallup

• This is the name, in their language, for the river along which they lived.

• Language: Salishan.

• The Puyallup lived at the mouth of the Puyallup River, the site of the present-day city of Seattle, Washington.

• There were 322 Puyallup in 1937 and 7,000 in 1985.

Quanah Parker
(1845-1911)

His name was *Quanah*, meaning "the perfumed one" and Parker, his mother's last name. Parker was of mixed race, the son of a white prisoner, Cynthia Parker, who was captured at age 12 in 1834, and Naw-Kohnee, the leader of the Kwahadi, the most aggressive of the COMANCHE. In 1874 he attacked a group of skinners (bison butchers) with a huge troop of 700 Kiowa and Comanche, and was then pursued for 2 years. Parker surrendered and encouraged his people to abandon intertribal wars and negoti-ate with the whites. He was persuaded that education was the route to his people's salvation, so he built SCHOOLS for young Indians and served as a mediator in numerous conflicts.

Quapaw

• They were the "downstream people" to their neighbors the Sioux. The Algonquian-language tribes called them the Arkansas. The French called them the "*Beaux hommes*," or "beautiful people."
• Language: Siouan, of the Dhegiha division.
• The Quapaw lived along the lower part of the Arkansas River, to which they gave their name.
• The Quapaw were semi-nomadic and farmed around their villages (corn, pumpkins, squash), hunted bear and deer, and followed the movements of the BISON herds.
• The Quapaw were in contact with Marquette in 1675 and with Cavelier de La Salle in 1682, then with the series of travelers who explored the Mississippi River. After suffering the consequences of invasions and of the decisions of the American government, they progres-

sively gave up their territory and moved to a reservation in Oklahoma.
• Many hundreds of Quapaw fought in France in 1917–1918.
• There were 2,500 Quapaw in 1650, 500 in 1829 and approximately 2,000 in 1990.

Quebec

The name of this beautiful Canadian province comes from the Micmac word *Kebec*, meaning "where the river narrows," which was the location of the city of the same name founded by Samuel de CHAMPLAIN in 1608.

Quileute

• A mispronunciation of their name *Quilayute*, the meaning of which is unknown.
• Language: Chimakuan, related to Nakashan and Salishan.
• The Quileute lived along the lower part of the Quilayute River, in northwestern Washington state.
• They were hunters and fishermen, including hunting SEALS and cetaceans like their neighbors and enemies to the north, the Makah.
• There were 500 Quileute in 1770, 284 in 1937, and 270 in 1970 on the La Push reservation.

Quinault

• A corruption of *Kwinail*.
• Language: Salishan.
• The Quinault lived at the mouth of the Quinault River in the southern part of the Quileute's territory in Washington state.
• The Quinault were hunters and fishermen. Like all the tribes of the northwest, the Quinault believed in a multitude of SPIRITS that were constantly involved in the human world. When the shaman tried to chase the evil spirit out of a sick person, he held a sculpted representation of his guiding spirit in his hand.
• In 1855, they gave up the majority of their lands in a treaty. Since then, they have lived on their lands on a reservation north of the city of Hoquiam. There were 719 Quinault in 1923, 1,228 in 1937, and 2,410 in 1995.

Quivira

The name of this mythical city is undoubtedly a Spanish corruption of *Kirikurus*, the name that the Pawnee called the Wichita. It was CORONADO's Pawnee guide who talked to him about this city with reportedly fabulous riches, in order to convince the Spaniard to travel north and become lost. The conquistador left with high hopes in the spring of 1591, but instead of the marvelous cities of gold, he found only poor Wichita villages.

Rabbits

Rabbits were an abundant game animal for the Indians across the entire area of the present-day United States. There are three species of rabbits: the cottontail (*Sylvilagus floridanus*), which was the smallest rabbit in the eastern half of the United States; the white-tailed jackrabbit (*Lepus townsendii*) in the Northwest; and the black-tailed jackrabbit (*Lepus californicus*) in the Southwest.

Raccoon

The American raccoon (*Procyon lotor*) lives on the forested banks of waterways. Its fur is also very sought after.

Rain in the Face
(1835-1905)

A Sioux chief who participated in the attack on the Fetterman colony and in the battle of LITTLE BIG HORN (1876), where he killed Tom Custer, General Custer's brother. His face was painted half red and half black, representing the sun and the darkness. One day, the rain made his war PAINT run, making lines on his face. It was from this incident that he took his name.

Raleigh
Walter (1552-1618)

After fighting alongside the Huguenots in France and the Netherlands, he was sent by Queen Elizabeth I of England to explore the unexplored areas of North America in 1584. He named the new lands Virginia, in honor of his sovereign, the "Virgin Queen." He pursued his adventurous life on the banks of the Orinoco and in Spain. After Elizabeth's death, Raleigh was involved in a plot, left again for Guyana, and upon the request of the Spanish, was arrested and decapitated.

Raven

Omnivorous bird that lives close to human civilizations, the raven is found throughout the entire North American continent except for the Arctic. It is likely that this is the reason that the Indians considered this animal an ally— since ravens (like COYOTES) warned them of coming danger or intruders. For the Indians of the Pacific Northwest, the raven played a leading role in their folklore: it is the "hero of transformation who is responsible for the natural order at the center of his universe, and it is he who brings light" (Martine J. Reid). The legend of the raven is represented on totem poles, symbolizing the culture of these peoples.

Red Cloud
(1822-1909)

Red Cloud was undoubtedly one of the greatest Sioux chiefs and one of the most notable personalities of the West. This DAKOTA Indian participated in all of the battles against the white invaders, endlessly winning back respect for Indian lands, forcing soldiers to leave and destroying their forts, notably the BOZEMAN trail. But he also understood before others did that in the face of the inequality of battle, it was preferable for the Indians to negotiate instead of surrender. In 1868 Red Cloud signed the treaty of Fort Laramie, Wyoming, but obstinately refused to give up the Black Hills. SITTING BULL, Red Cloud's former accomplice in battle, reproached him for what he saw as a compromise. In 1874 the discovery of gold in the Black Hills led to the de facto nullification of the treaty. Red Cloud was forcibly moved to the Pine Ridge reservation and died there in 1909.

Red Jacket
(1756-1830)

His actual name was Segoyawatha. This SENECA chief was thus nicknamed because he always wore a red jacket. He was allied with the English against the Americans. Subsequent to a law forbidding whites from staying on Indian reservations, he insisted that the missionaries leave, "Because they don't bring us anything truly good, and serve only to make our people depressed and feeling constantly guilty for something, and we don't want this. If they are not useful to the whites, then why send them to us?"

Reservations

Reservations were recommended beginning in 1800 by President JEFFERSON, who was convinced that the Indians could become sedentary farmers and thus integrate into white society. Work being the source of all virtues, the idea was carried out: From Texas to California, the Indians were despoiled of their lands and put onto reservations administered by the federal authorities. The measure was even more attractive because its application freed up land. The Indians thus became the victims of a vast system of corruption maintained by land speculators and provisions suppliers from the Bureau of Indian Affairs. Beginning with his election in 1869, Ulysses GRANT attempted to make order out of this chaos and, in order to accomplish the desired integration, mobilized religious authorities; the elite of Boston, Philadelphia, and New York (Indian Rights Association); and feminist associations (Women's National Indian Association). It was no longer a question of integration but of assimilation: This involved the prohibition of certain aspects of Indian culture (shamanism, polygamy, initiation and funeral rites, etc). The Dawes Act of 1887 authorized the dismantling of reservations through attribution of a parcel of 160 acres to each Indian family. Many of these new owners gave up their land for laughable sums of money, much to the delight of the speculators. The Dawes Act also enabled the opening of OKLA-HOMA to colonists, completely dismantling the positive efforts of the FIVE CIVILIZED NATIONS, who had organized their own government and school system. Thus, the policy of assimilation failed for the 248,253 Indians of the 1890 census and for their descendants. But, paradoxically, reservations undoubtedly saved the Indians from total extinction and opened possibilities for a true renewal.

Rice

A variety called "wild rice" (*Zizania aquatica*) constituted the primary resource for the Indians who lived on the banks of lakes Superior and Michigan (Ojibwa, Menominee, Winnebago). The harvest was carried out by canoe at the end of summer. During the harvesting procedure, a large part of the rice grains fell into the water, thus ensuring future germination. The harvested rice was dried in the sun and the wind took care of winnowing it. Wild rice was eaten boiled, sometimes mixed with meat or with maple syrup added to it.

Roadrunner

Also known as the California cuckoo, the roadrunner (*Geococcyx californi-*

anus) is a running bird that is specific to the southwestern region. Even when it is surprised to be discovered, the roadrunner can flee thanks to quick changes of direction. It is partial to insects, lizards, scorpions, and other small snakes. In the Sonora, Chihuahua, or Mojave Deserts, the coyote is its most common predator, but it is nevertheless unlucky, if we're to believe a cartoon series ("Beep Beep").

Roman Nose
(1830-1868)

A CHEYENNE chief and Dog Soldier warrior, famous for his athletic build. A contemporary of DULL KNIFE, he carried on a constant battle against the white colonists, notably the Mormons. He tried to prevent the opening of the Bozeman Trail. Roman Nose died on the banks of the Arickaree River during a raid against a troop corps led by General Forsyth.

Rosebud

On this site near Yellowstone, one of the largest battles of the Indian wars took place on June 17, 1876. It opposed the forces of General CROOK (2,500 men, reinforced by 250 Crow and Shoshone scouts) against the Sioux and Cheyenne led by SITTING BULL and CRAZY HORSE. The outcome of the battle was indecisive, but the Indians earned a psychological victory, since Crook decided to return to his bases. Five days later, General Custer took the initiative to finish off the Indian resistance and penetrated into the LITTLE BIG HORN Valley.

Sitting Bull

Rushes

A basic material for the Indians of the Great Basin and California (used for basket weaving, shelters, small boats, etc). The Indians used two varieties that are native to the New World, *Scirpus californicus* and *Scirpus acutus*.

S

Sacajawea

(1786-1812)

A famous SHOSHONE woman who accompanied the LEWIS and CLARK expedition (1804–1806) as an interpreter. She had been kidnapped as a child and then raised by the Hidatsa, who sold her to Toussaint Charbonneau, a Canadian "woods runner" (trapper) who lived among the Hidatsa, where her name means "bird woman." She perfectly fulfilled her role as interpreter and guide in the service of the two explorers and returned with her son to her tribe's reservation. According to certain sources, she died not in 1812 but in 1884 at the age of almost 100.

Sachem

This word of Seneca origin referred to hereditary honor (chiefship) in the Algonquin tribes of Massachusetts. Thus, the League of Five Iroquois Nations was directed by a counsel of fifty sachems who had decision-making and advisory power over all of the major questions related to tribal life: peace and war, alliances, seasonal migrations, justice, and so on.

Salish

- Numerous Salishan-language groups occupied the islands and coasts of the north Pacific region: Bella Coola, Comox, Nanaimo, Klallam, Nisqualli, Puyallup, Skagit. They traded actively with the Salish who lived in the interior.
- The most numerous and influential were undoubtedly the Cowichans, who settled in the southeastern part of Vancouver Island.

Salishan

See Languages, pg. 14.

175

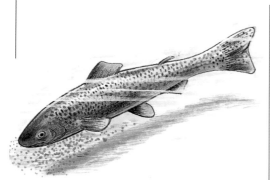

Salmon

Many species of salmonidae populate the rivers of the Pacific coast. The chinook salmon (*Oncorhynchus tshawytscha*) are among the most common. It is also a very sought-after catch for anglers, along with sockeye salmon (*Oncorhynchus nerka*) and coho salmon (*Oncorhynchus kitsutch*).

In the month of April, the Indians left their winter camps and moved near rivers where they settled during fairer weather. Fishing sites were carefully located and prepared to trap or harpoon the maximum amount of fish coming up toward their spawning areas. The narrowest passages were dug out and lined with white stones and gravel to make it easier to see the furtive sparkling of the fish that were swimming upstream. In certain locations that lent themselves to harpooning, the Indians built wooden balance lines; in other places they built dams or bridges that crossed above the rapids. Fishing continued throughout the summer until the end of the spawning period.

The Pacific coast, Oregon

Sand Creek

On November 29, 1864, despite the fact that Chief Black Kettle had met with President Lincoln to establish peace, and while the CHEYENNE camp flew both the star-spangled banner (indicating American support) and a white flag (indicating surrender), 700 men from the U.S. Cavalry led by Colonel Chivington descended on Sand Creek, Colorado, and massacred more than 500 people, including women and children. This odious killing spawned a wave of indignation in the country, but motivated all of the tribes to join the Cheyenne in their desire for revenge.

Sanspoil

• Corruption of an Indian word of unknown meaning.
• Language: Salishan.
• Lived along the Sanspoil and Nespelem rivers in northeastern Washington State.
• There is a reservation on their territory: 800 inhabitants in 1780, 202 in 1913.

Santee

"The river is there." One of the divisions of the Dakota Sioux.

Sarcee

• Sa-arsi: "bad" in Blackfoot.
• Language: Athabascan.

• Lived along the Saskatchewan and Athabasca rivers in Alberta, Canada. These semi-nomads of the north Great Plains hunted BISON.
• The Sarcee suffered greatly from the aggressiveness of the Cree and other tribes before being hard-hit by epidemics: smallpox (1836 and 1870) and scarlet fever (1856). Under the leadership of their chief Bull Head, they fought to obtain a viable reservation near Calgary (1879–1881).
• The Sarcee numbered 700 in 1670 and 400 in 1938.

Satanta
(1830–1878)

A KIOWA chief and great orator, he signed the Medicine Lodge treaty in 1867 but didn't lessen his pursuit of murderous raids against the colonists. On the warpath in 1874, he was arrested by CUSTER and committed suicide in prison, at least according to the official version.

Sauk

• An abbreviation of their name *Asakiwaki*, meaning "people of the yellow earth." They were mentioned by the Jesuits in 1640 under the Huron name *Hvattoghronon*, meaning "people of the west."
• Language: Algonquian.
• Settled near Lake Michigan, in the eastern part of the present-day state of Wisconsin.

• The Sauk were farmers (corn, beans and squash) and hunted bison and other large game. They were semi-nomadic like their allies the FOX. They used and traded lead, which was abundant in the region. They were reputed to be among the most warlike of the Great Lakes region.

• They were successively adversaries of the French, English, and Americans and participated in the revolts of Pontiac in 1763 and Tecumseh, between 1801 and 1814. The Sauk signed a treaty in 1815, which ratified the loss of their lands. In 1832 they threw themselves into one last revolt that was doomed to failure, under the leadership of their chief BLACK HAWK. The revot was opposed by another one of their chiefs, KEOKUK, who worked to maintain good relations with the American government.

• Their descendants live in reservations in Oklahoma (with the Fox) and in Iowa. Together, they numbered 1,842 in 1985.

Scalp

The Indians of the northeast practiced scalping before the arrival of the Europeans. The Indian who won a battle thought that by scalping his victim, he could steal his victim's life force and prevent the victim from finding peace in the afterlife. The whites imitated this practice and scalped the Indians that they killed, especially when the authorities offered bounties in exchange for concrete proof. In the eigtheenth century, the practice of scalping spread throughout the entire continent, in particular on the Great Plains. The Sioux, Crow, and Blackfeet were eager to hang these gruesome trophies on their HORSES, SHIELDS, or leggings.

School

The school of life and the school of nature were the only school that Indian children knew. At the end of the nineteenth century, the American government decided to open schools for children who lived on reservations. This initiative satisfied two goals: integrating the youngest Indians into American society and reducing cultural heritage that the surviving adults on reservations were attempting to preserve. More than 4,000 children from about a dozen tribes were taken into the Carlisle Indian School in Pennsylvania between 1875 and 1918, where they

179

were subjected to severe discipline. Other schools of this type were opened, but the experience didn't give the results that had been anticipated; in fact, it led to a twofold rejection: a rejection of the culture of origin by some, and a rejection of the integration plan by most. On the reservations, other schools were opened with Indian teachers. In 1913, 78 percent of Amerindian children were enrolled in school.

Scout

The Union armies used numerous Indian scouts during the wars of the nineteenth century. They recruited them from tribes that were traditional enemies of the tribes who opposed the "blue coats." The APACHE, PAWNEE, and

Apache scout

CROW were thus the most numerous to help the army in its merciless fight against the Dakota and Cheyenne.

Sculpture

The pre-Columbian cultures (Adena, Hopewell, Hohokam, Mogollon, Anasazi) left artifacts demonstrating the taste and talents of the people who

Kwakiutl mask

lived in these bygone eras; they sculpted small statuettes and decorative or useful objects. The Indians of the sixteenth century hadn't abandoned this activity, as the first European travelers saw; the Calusa were skilled sculptors of wooden objects and, in other regions, artists sculpted pipes, masks, and containers. The most remarkable creations were those of the tribes inhabiting the north-west coast (Haida, Tlingit, Tsimshian, Kwakiutl). Using red cedar wood, these tribes made TOTEMS, masks, MUSIC instruments, furniture, PIPES, and WEAPONS. Further to the north, the Inuit had a real talent for producing small ivory sculptures to ward off walruses.

Seal

The seal (*Phoca hispida*) is present throughout the Arctic zone from Alaska to Labrador and Newfoundland. It can stay submerged for more than 20 minutes, but most often it comes back to the surface to breathe every 3 minutes, using holes that it digs in the ice. Like bison for the Plains Indians, the seal supplied all elements essential to INUIT life.

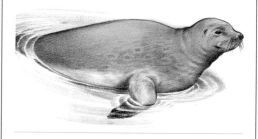

Secotan

• Means "there where it is burned," which may be an allusion to this farming people's technique of clearing brush by burning.

• Language: Algonquian.
• They settled along the coast of North Carolina, between Albemarle Bay and Pamlico Bay.
• They were farmers (corn, beans, squash), but they also hunted and fished. Their villages, near the ocean, were surrounded by barriers: They included ten to thirty large houses.
• Their life was described by John White, who accompanied Sir Walter

The Seminole raised cows using animals that had been abandoned by the Spanish.

• An INTERBRED people composed of successive infusions of Indians fleeing the progression of whites (Yamassee, Apalachee, Red Stick Creek) and black slaves. From 1817 to 1858, three wars against the Americans forced the Seminole to progressively leave Florida. Led by the brilliant chief OSCEOLA, they fought without any assistance. This was a merciless battle in the swamps and

Raleigh. They were, like their neighbors the POWHATAN, overwhelmed by European colonization in the seventeenth century. The Machapunga, Pamlico, and Hatteras tribes who later lived in the region appear to be the descendants of the Secotan.

Seminole

• May be the translation of a Creek term meaning "fleeting." More likely a corruption of the Spanish word *cimarron*, meaning "savage." The Seminole called themselves *Ikaniuksalgi*, "people of the peninsula."
• Language: Muskogean.
• Settled in Florida.
• They were farmers (corn, squash, tobacco, sweet potatoes, melons), hunters, fishermen, and fruit gatherers.

Seneca

See Iroquois.

Sequoyah
(1770–1843)

The son of a white man and a CHEROKEE woman, Sequoyah invented an alphabet that allowed his people to read and write. To honor him, the California great red pine was given his name, but with a phonetic spelling (Sequoia).

Serrano

- Means "highlander" in Spanish.
- Language: Shoshonean.
- Settled east of the present-day city of Los Angeles.
- Converted to Christianity very early on, and settled in small isolated villages in California. These Indians lived by hunting and gathering (acorns, grasses).
- There were 1,500 in 1770, 118 in 1910, 1,085 in 1985.

Shaman

See Medicine man.

Shasta

- Name of unknown origin.
- Language: Hokan.
- Lived in the border zone between California and Oregon. Confined to a reservation with inhospitable soil, they almost completely disappeared.

jungle, which cost the U.S. Army the lives of more than 1,500 soldiers. But the Indians, overwhelmed by the number and weaponry of the army, had to give up. Aside from 300 Seminole who refused to leave the EVERGLADES, the others (approximately 3,000) went into exile.

- In 1990 there were 13,800 Seminole in Oklahoma, Arkansas, and Florida. Most of them converted to Christianity. They live in their thatch dwellings and still make their famous multicolor patchwork shirts and dresses.

- They numbered 2,000 in 1770 and 100 in 1910.

Shawnee

- From the Algonquin *Shawun*, "the south."
- Language: Algonquian.
- Lived in the Ohio Valley, then, at the end of the seventeenth century, migrated in two directions. Some went to Pennsylvania, close to their allies the DELAWARE, and others to Georgia and Alabama where they would be known by the name Sawagoni.

- Sedentary farmers and hunters. Their fields and orchards were fenced, and their villages were well organized. The Shawnee were known for their courage, happiness, and good sense.
- Tenaciously fought against the English, then against the American colonists. Their great chief TECUMSEH inflicted defeat upon the Americans in the battle of WABASH on November 4, 1791. But, under the direction of General Wayne, the Americans took their revenge at Fallen Timbers. Despite the prophecies of Tecumseh's brother Tenskwatawa, the Shawnee were definitively beaten in 1813. Twenty years later, they were deported beyond the Mississippi. Their descendants live on a reservation in Oklahoma. There were 3,000 in 1650, 916 in 1937, 1,039 in 1944.

Sheridan
Philip Henry
(1831-1888)

An American general, he was one of the leaders on the winning side of the Civil War. In 1868, Sheridan asked CUSTER to attack the Cheyenne camp of Washita. He became commander in chief of the Union armies in 1884. He is credited with coining a sadly famous sentence, "The only good Indian is a dead Indian." According to some, he actually said, "The only good Indians I ever knew were dead," which might have a different meaning. According to others, the quotation dated from Pontiac's war, and its author was James Cavanaugh, who represented Montana in Congress.

Sherman
William Tecumseh
(1820-1891)

An American general and another great winner of the Civil War. He was one of the signers of the FORT LARAMIE treaty in November 1868. As commander of the Union armies from 1866 to 1884, he carried out countless campaigns against the Plains tribes. He was most notably one of the first to understand that more than weapons, the ever-growing number of colonists threatened the Indians. This is why he encouraged the construction of railroads and invited "all of the hunters in North America and Great Britain" to come shoot bison, always moving westward.

Shields

To protect himself during combat, the Indian warrior owns a shield: made of wood, or in the case of the Plains Indians, bison leather taken from the scapula where the hide is thickest. Shields that were, at times, made of two thicknesses of leather proved to be so resistant that lead bullets could not penetrate them. Most shields were painted decoratively and adorned with feathers and scalps.

Shoshone

• Name of uncertain origin. Might mean "in the valley." Some neighboring tribes had names for the Shoshone in their own languages such as "those who live in grass huts," but for the most part, they were the "snakes," or the "snake people."
• Language: Shoshonean.
• The Northern Shoshone lived in eastern Idaho, western Wyoming, and northeastern Utah, near the Great Salt Lake. The Western Shoshone were found from western to southern Idaho, in southwestern Utah and northern Nevada.
• The Northern Shoshone lived, like the Plains Indians, off the bison hunt. They introduced the HORSE to many

185

SHO

Shoshonean

See Languages, pg. 15.

Shupwap

- Meaning unknown
- Language: Salishan.
- Lived in southern British Columbia between the Fraser and Columbia Rivers.
- Alexander MACKENZIE encountered them in 1793 as did Simon Fraser in 1808. They were then in contact with fur traders from the Hudson Bay Company in 1816, then with miners, and they were progressively chased off their land. They numbered 220 in 1950.

Siksika

See Blackfeet.

Siouan

See Languages, pg. 14.

Sioux

See Dakota.

Sitting Bull
(1830-1890)

The Hunkpapa Sioux's war chief and MEDICINE MAN, Sitting Bull, born Tatanka Iyotanka, was the most famous of the great Indian chiefs and the symbol of

Sitting Bull, photograph by D.F. Barry, 1885

neighboring tribes: Blackfeet, Crow, Nez Perce. The Western Shoshone were more sedentary and devoted themselves primarily to gathering and salmon fishing.

- In constant conflict with their neighbors, the Shoshone understood before their neighbors did that white victory was inevitable. Having even supplied the "blue coats" with SCOUTS, they obtained the superb Wind River RESERVATION in Wyoming.
- Numbering approximately 4,500 in 1845, the Shoshone number 9,000 today, with a high rate of racial mixing.

resistance against the invader. He achieved his first "coup" at the age of 14, against the Crow. Over the years, he earned his status as a strategist and wise man and imposed his leadership on all of the Sioux and their allies, the Cheyenne. In a dream, he had a vision of the battles of ROSEBUD and LITTLE BIG HORN (1876) and predicted their violence and outcomes. From that day forth, despite the success of his Indian forces over General Custer's seventh cavalry regiment, he refused to approve of other battles, persuaded by the conviction that against the white colonists, whose numbers grew every year, the Indians couldn't win. After leaving for exile in Canada with his people, Sitting Bull agreed to return to the United States upon the promise that his people would be treated well (1881), but he was captured on his return, out of fear that he would provoke a new uprising, and brought to the Standing Rock reservation. In 1885 he became an attraction at Buffalo Bill's Wild West show. He returned to Standing Rock, where another dream predicted his murder by his own people. In 1890 he was assassinated by two Indians who were paid by the army. The assassins were also killed in turn, some time after their heinous crime.

Skagit
- Meaning unknown.
- Language: Salishan.
- Lived along the middle part of the Skagit and Stillaguamish Rivers (in Washington state).

- There were 1,200 in 1780, 200 in 1957, and 259 in 1970.

Skitswish
- Means "those who are found here." They were also called the *Cour d'Alène* ("heart of an awl") by the French.
- Language: Salishan.
- Lived along the upper part of the Spokane River and around Lake Coeur d'Alène (Washington State, east of the city of Spokane, straddling the border with Idaho).
- There were 1,000 in 1780, 608 (with the Spokan) in 1937 on a reservation on their lands.

Slave
- Their actual name was the *Etchaottines*, "those who live in a shelter." They suffered the domination of their neighbors the Cree, who called them *Awokanac*, meaning "slaves."
- Language: Athabascan.
- Lived in the valley of the Mackenzie River, west of Great Slave Lake.
- There were 1,250 in 1670 and 3,004 in 1967.

Sleigh
To travel over snow, the INUIT built sleighs. The materials used were wood, cetacean bones, or caribou antlers. Inuit sleighs could reach 13 feet (4 meters) in length; husky dogs, under the direction of a leader, pulled the sleighs.

Smallpox

Beginning with the first contacts between whites and Indians, the Indians were contaminated by viruses against which they were not immunized. Smallpox EPIDEMICS were by far the most deadly, cutting the Great Plains population in half during the nineteenth century alone. Sometimes caused by the distribution of contaminated blankets, these epidemics ravaged sedentary tribes such as the Mandan in particular.
See Epidemics.

Smith

John (1579-1631)

An English navigator and colonizer who landed in Chesapeake Bay with some 100 men (1607), he led three expeditions in Virginia and founded Jamestown (1609). After being taken prisoner by the Indians, POCAHONTAS saved his life. But far from diffusing

the tensions between the two communities, this noble gesture led to other extortions and new massacres.

Snake

The North American continent is rich in a great variety of snakes. They are rarer in the north, but their population is particularly dense in the south. Many, like grass snakes, are not at all dangerous, but the number of dangerous species is larger than in Europe. This is not a complete list, but we will list some dangerous snakes:
• the coral snake of the south coast and Arizona;
• the copperhead, present in all of the Southeast, extending to Texas;

Northern Pacific Rattlesnake

Diamondback Rattlesnake

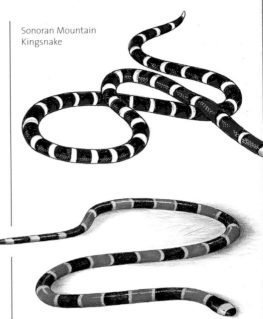

Sonoran Mountain Kingsnake

Coral snake

• all rattlesnakes. Some, such as the timber rattler, can reach 6 feet (1.8 meters) in length. All rattlesnakes can cause deadly bites: the blacktail, tiger, sidewinder, red diamond, and diamondback rattlesnakes. Rattlesnakes are present in forests, along ponds, in deserts . . . everywhere!

Snake

Nickname given to many tribes for reasons that we can imagine. Either this is a term of contempt for a miserable condition (the Walpapi of Oregon were called Snakes and the Southern Paiute were called Snake diggers), or a term denoting the dangerousness of warriors (as with the COMANCHE and the SHOSHONE), or more simply because they lived in a region where the population of reptiles was particularly dense (true of all regions of the West). For purposes of comparison, the IROQUOIS, who were fierce warriors, were nicknamed the Nadowa (Vipers) by their Algonquin enemies.

Snowsnake

A Seneca game consisting of throwing a 5 to 8 foot (1.5 to 2.5 meter) wooden (hickory, walnut, willow, or maple) pole into a small trench dug in the snow. The trench could be as large as 1,640 feet (500 meters) long by 1.3 feet (40 centimeters) deep.

Societies

Societies brought men or women together for every important activity: war, religion, dancing and singing, artistic activities. Each individual could simultaneously belong to many societies, according to his or her various functions in the tribe. Certain societies were welcoming, others were closed, meaning that they were secret (such as the HAMATSA society of the Kwakiutl tribe of the Pacific coast). Warrior societies were particularly important for the Plains people.

We can identify two types:
• Graded societies were structured by age category (Blackfoot, Arapaho, Mandan, Hidatsa) where every person could successively progress

up the different levels, from neophytes of 15 or 20 years old to the oldest and most honored warriors. When the young Indians thought themselves sufficiently experienced to enter into the warrior hierarchy, they had to purchase their rights from members of the first level, their immediate elders. This led to gifts and festivities. Dispossessed of

Dog Soldier (Cheyenne)

their prerogatives (songs, dances, ceremonies, rites), the "sellers" then had
as their legitimate ambition to reach
the next level. Following specific rites,
groups of warriors thus passed from
one level to another. The progression
up the hierarchy preserved the homo-
geneity of age and experience in
the eight to 12 levels depending on
the tribe.
• Nongraded societies competed within
one tribe (Teton Sioux, Crow,
Cheyenne, Assiniboine, Omaha, Ponca).
The rules were almost identical for all of
the societies, but the extent to which
they were known varied. Although
there was no discrimination against
those who joined the ranks, the overall
value or the exploits of an exceptional
warrior meant a great deal to ensure the
supremacy of a society. Thus, competition for attracting the most valiant
stayed alive, and anything was fair
game when it came to picking fights
and confronting each other on the field.
The desire to one-up each other in
terms of bravery led the members of
certain societies (the Teton Sioux's
Miwa'tani or the famous Cheyenne DOG
SOLDIERS) to tie themselves, using a wide
belt, to a stake driven into the battle
field, so that they were obliged to win
or die. "Contrary" warriors (the
Cheyenne Bow String society) pushed
the bounds of courage even further:
Doing the contrary of what logic dic-
tated (yes for no, go forward for retreat),
they refused to join the battle if their
brothers in arms were winners, but

eagerly participated in the case of an
overwhelming defeat. WOMEN could also
be involved in societies, either as possible warriors (Cheyenne) or for their skill
in certain activities (for example, work
done with porcupine spines in the
Cheyenne, Mandan, or Hidatsa tribes).

Spirits
The Indians' invisible world is populated by the spirits, and most of all by
the *Great Spirit*. During rituals and ceremonies, the Great Spirit was asked to
give a sign of which path to take. The
Algonquian-language peoples called
the Great Spirit MANITOU; the Iroquois,
Orenda; the Sioux nations Wakanda or
Wakan Tanka. The protector Spirit, who
accompanies and protects each person,
and all of the spirits who occupy the
plant, and especially the animal world,
are also honored. In the image of
humans, the spirits are part of the natural order of the universe and have their
own role to play in it.

Spokan
• Etymology uncertain. Might mean
"people of the sun."
• Language: Salishan.
• Settled in the eastern part of
Washington state.
• Fished and hunted all types of game
including BISON.
• Resisted the American army for 2
years, until the Fort Elliot treaty in
1855.

he kept his word. Named by the government as chief of all RESERVATIONS, he learned English. But Spotted Tail was criticized for his relations with the whites and Crow Dog assassinated him near the Rosebud reservation.

Squaw

An Algonquin word meaning "woman." This was used in English then in French to denote an Indian wife, whatever tribe she belonged to. This term, judged to be pejorative, is no longer used by today's communities.

Squirrel

Many species of squirrels populated the forests of North America, from the flying squirrel (*Glaucomys sablinus*) to the different types of chipmunks or ground squirrels (*Eutamias umbrinus, E. townsendii, minimus*, etc.) along

• Their descendants live on reservations in Montana and Washington. The Spokan numbered approximately 2,000 circa 1780, 847 in 1937, and 1,961 in 1990.

Spotted Tail
(1823-1881)

Brulé Sioux chief who earned his title for his bravery in battle . . . or for his habit of wearing raccoon tails as decorations on his outfit. He chose the path of war in 1854, attacked trains and convoys, but was beaten, captured, and sentenced to death. Pardoned under the condition of not taking up arms again, with the red and gray varieties (*Tamiasciurus hudsonicus, Sciurus griseus*).

Subarctic

See Indian Lands, pg. 8.

Sun Dance

Under the shaman's direction, the Sun Dance was a ceremony dedicated to the Great Spirit (Wakan Tanka) to give thanks for the kindnesses given forth by Nature. The bison was also honored as the very symbol of life. In the shelter of a dance lodge built for the occasion, the Sun Dance happened in summer; with some variations, it was common to all the tribes of the Great Plains. It lasted from 8 to 12 days with alternating festivities and self-mutilation tests for warriors. The participants committed to fasting completely and danced from sunrise to sunset, always facing the sun.

On the last day, they pierced their chests with a hook that was tied to the end of a cord which was itself tied to the Tree of Life, a poplar placed at the center of the ceremonial area. Or, the dancers might be pierced in the back and pull bison skulls behind them while they danced, until their flesh ripped and freed them from their restraints. Thus, harmony between all living beings was guaranteed.

Susqehannock

- Meaning unknown
- Language: Iroquoian.
- Lived along the Susquehanna River (in Delaware, Pennsylvania, and Maryland).
- There were 5,000 in 1600. They disappeared around 1770, victims of the Iroquois and of white extortion.

Sweat lodge

The sweat lodge (*Onikaghe*, meaning "renewal of life") is a major part of Indian life. This is where an Indian comes for purification before a ceremony or before leaving for battle. But the sweat lodge may also be used very frequently, even daily, for no reason other than hygiene: this was the case for the Kiowa, Arapahoe, and Cheyenne. The lodge was a dome of animal skins stretched over a frame made of willow branches. Inside the lodge, there was a hole for hot rocks, on which water was poured in order to produce hot steam. After a half hour or more in this atmosphere, the Indians would dive into a nearby river and rub themselves with herbs. The practice of sweating was one of the methods used to cure diseases or to lose oneself in deep meditation. Some initiates came to the sweat lodge to seek VISIONS that were a source of explanations for the order of the universe or crucial aids in making major decisions.

T

Tahltan

- Meaning unknown.
- Language: Athabascan.
- Settled around the border of British Columbia, where they fished on the Stikine River, and the Yukon.
- The Tahltan were caribou and moose hunters and according to their own legend were the result of the combination of many tribes from different areas and languages other than Athabascan. Very close with the coastal TLINGIT, their environment was disrupted by successive arrivals of GOLD seekers after 1874. They also suffered smallpox EPIDEMICS in 1864 and 1868.
- The Tahltan numbered 1,000 in 1780 and 229 in 1909.

Taiga

In the Subarctic region, a zone occupied by a vast forest of conifers and silver birch. The taiga, south of the polar tundra, covers the same latitude in Asia and Europe and takes its name from the Russian word for this forest.

Tamaroa

See Illinois.

Tanana

- Long referred to as the *Tenan-Kutchin*, "people of the mountain," and wrongly considered to be one of the Kutchin tribes. However, they bear the name of the Tanana River, a tributary of the Yukon River.
- Language: Athabascan.
- Lived along the lower part of the Tanana River (Alaska).

- Proud warriors and feared by their neighbors, they were also known for the quality of the ornamentation on their parkas. They were great CARIBOU hunters.
- Numbered 415 individuals in 1910. Earlier estimates are uncertain. According to the *Tanano Chiefs Conference*, they numbered 7,039 in 1985.

Tanoan
See Languages, pg. 15.

Tattoos
Tattooing was a widespread practice among the Indians. Tattoos could be simply decorative (peoples of the Atlantic coast and the Great Lakes, the Wichita of the Great Plains), but they could also have other significance of a social or sacred nature, related to the totemic powers of the person or the tribe (Haida).

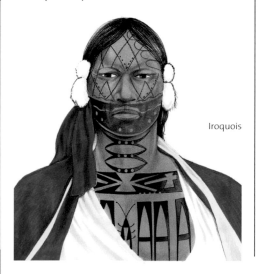

Iroquois

- For the Inuit, a tattoo marked the passage to puberty or marriage for women. For men, it was their skill as a hunter that was thus signified.
- A specific function in the tribe (guardian of the sacred pipe for the Osage) or a role as liaison with the spirits (Hupa) justified a tattoo.
- Kiowa women were tattooed with a circle on their foreheads; for the Omaha, the same symbol or a four-pointed star on the breast symbolized the ties between a daughter and her parents.
- Certain tattoos were supposed to prevent illnesses (for the Chippewa, toothaches).

Tattoos were a pretext for ceremonies, accompanied by songs and dances, and an expert from the tribe was responsible for the procedure using needles (fragments of metal or plant spines) and charcoal-based ink. In 1530, Cabeza de Vaca mentioned blue and red tattoos in the tribes of the Gulf of Mexico.

Tecumseh
(1768-1813)
Famous SHAWNEE chief, whose name meant "he who crosses from one point to another" or more simply "shooting star." With the help of his brother Tenskwatawa, he tried to unify the peoples from Ohio to Florida, convinced that this was the only way of effectively countering the whites' insatiable appetite for new lands. But his efforts were in vain: defeated at the battle of Fallen Timbers (1794),

Tecumseh went into exile in Canada and joined the British troops against the United States. In battle once again, he was killed on October 5, 1813, in the Battle of the Thames, near the present-day city of Chatam, Ontario, Canada.

Teton

Means "those who live on the prairie." They constituted the Lakota division (Lakota = Dakota, but pronounced differently).
See Dakota.

Tewa

• "Moccasins."
• Language: Tanoan.
• PUEBLO people settled in northern New Mexico, they were divided into two branches: north of Santa Fe in the

Rio Chama Valley; south of Santa Fe in the Rio Grande Valley (these were also called Tano).
• Targeted by the APACHE's attacks, they were then severely tested during the Pueblo revolt between 1680 and 1696. The Tewa then suffered SMALLPOX epidemics in the nineteenth century.
• In the north, there were 2,200 in 1680, 968 in 1910.
• In the south, there were 4,000 in 1630. In 1930, all of them (north and south) numbered 3,412 individuals.

Thompson

• Name given by the whites, in reference to the Thompson River. The tribe called itself *Ntlakyapamuk* (meaning unknown).
• Language: Salishan.
• Valleys of the Thompson and Fraser Rivers (British Columbia), a mountainous region covered with forests.
• Fished for SALMON and hunted (caribou, fallow deer, moose). Their semi-underground log houses were covered with earth.
• Very structured society, often under group direction. Around the time of puberty, each boy underwent a "VISION quest" test, where he went

alone into the mountains to search for his guardian spirit.
Were particularly decimated by the invasion of their territory by miners (1858) and by SMALLPOX epidemics in subsequent years.
• The Thompson continue to live on narrow parcels. Possibly numbering 5,000 circa 1780, 1,776 were counted in 1906. Today they are 6,000 individuals, of which half live on reservations. In their schools, they encourage the learning of their ancestral language.

Tillamook

• "People of the Nehalem River" in Chinook.
• Language: Salishan.
• Lived on the Pacific coast, between the Salmon and Nehalem Rivers (northwestern Oregon).
• Fished almost exclusively.
• They numbered 2,200 in 1805 and 12 in 1930.

Timucua

• Also known by the name *Utina*, "chiefs." Timucua probably meant ruler or master.
• Language: Muskogean.
• Settled in the northern part of Florida.
• Farmers, hunters, and fishermen, the Timucua lived in round houses grouped in fortified villages. Very skilled sailors, they traded with Cuba.
• Encountered successively by Ponce de Léon (1513), Narvaez (1528), de Soto

(1539), and Ribault (1562). The Spanish supplanted the French and Christianized the Timucua before the Timucua were decimated by the Creek, the Yuchi, and the Catawba, assisted by the English.
• There were 13,000 Timucua in 1650, they no longer existed a century later.

Tionontati

• Means "there where the mountain is." They were also called "tobacco people" or *Tabaccos* by the French.
• Language: Iroquoian.

199

- Lived north of Lake Erie.
- Visited by the French in 1616; the Jesuits established a mission among them in 1640. The Tionontati welcomed the Huron, who were victims of the Iroquois of the League of Five Nations, but they too were attacked by the Iroquois. They left their region and found refuge with the Huron in the Ohio Valley.
- They numbered 8,000 in 1600. Since then, they were integrated into the Huron total.

Tipi

Shelter of the nomadic Indians of the Great Plains, from the Lakota word for "dwelling." Tipis belonged to WOMEN, who assembled and disassembled them very rapidly. According to the tribes, they were erected with three or four base poles, to which were added some twenty supporting posts holding tanned, treated, and layered bison skins. In the middle of the nineteenth century, canvas often replaced the skins. Oriented to the east to shelter the occupants from dominant winds, tipis had an opening at the top to let out smoke. On the contrary, when the weather was good, the sides were raised to air out the interior. Most were comfortable: soft furs and fragrant brush covered the floor. Set up at the beginning of the summer for clan meetings, the Counsel tipi could reach 26 feet (8 meters) high and 39 feet (12 meters) in diameter. The very particular painted tipis belonged to shamans and healers. Their designs evoked the visions of the shelter's occupant.

Tlingit

- Name derived from *Lingit*, "people."
- Linguistic isolate.

- Occupied the islands of the Alexander Archipelago within Alaska.
- They were SALMON fishermen, sculptors, and basket weavers, as well as active and prosperous traders and feared warriors. The ocean's resources (fish, shellfish, whale bones, and oil) freed them from practicing agriculture.
- Like most of the coastal tribes, the Tlingit observed family lineage through WOMEN. A father was responsible for

201

the education of his sister's children while his own children depended on the authority of the wife's brother. Girls had to remain celibate until marriage. The passage from childhood to womanhood was accompanied by rigorous and demanding rites: an absolute fast for many days, total immobility in a sitting position in a hut apart from the village, rubbing of the face with a hard stone and piercing of the lower lip.
• Expanding population: 10,000 in 1750, 14,000 in 1990.

Tobacco

From the Guarani word *Tobacco*. To the Indians, tobacco was a sacred plant. They believed that its use made it possible to prevent illnesses and call on the good SPIRITS, meaning communicating with them. In the narrative that Christopher Columbus wrote about his travels, he confirmed this use by the peoples that he had met. The plant's dried leaves were mixed with other plant matter: laurel or MAPLE leaves; dogwood, cherry, willow, poplar, or birch bark. The mixture varied depending on the tribe and region, and was called *kinnikinnik* (from the Algonquian word *kinnick*, "to mix").

Tomahawk

A name which, in different variations (*tommattick, tomohack, tommyhawk, tomahigan*), designates the same type of weapon in the Algonquin tribes. The name was adopted for multiple types of clubs used from one end of the continent to the other. The tomahawk is made of wood, horn or bone, artistically decorated or sculpted, and might or might not have a round or pointed stone, or a metal blade. Beginning at the end of the eighteenth century, stone was replaced with a metal blade, and a type made in Europe combined an axe and a PIPE, and could function in war or for the pleasure of smoking.

Tonkawa

• Means "they are together."
• A linguistic isolate linked to Karankawan.
• Lived in southeastern Texas.
• In the eighteenth century, they were allied with the Comanche and the Wichita against the looting Apache. Attempts at MISSIONS to convert them were abandoned in 1756. Later, epidemics and confrontations with the Caddo, Shawnee, Wichita, and the Oklahoma Delaware definitively weakened them.

TOMAHAWKS AND CLUBS

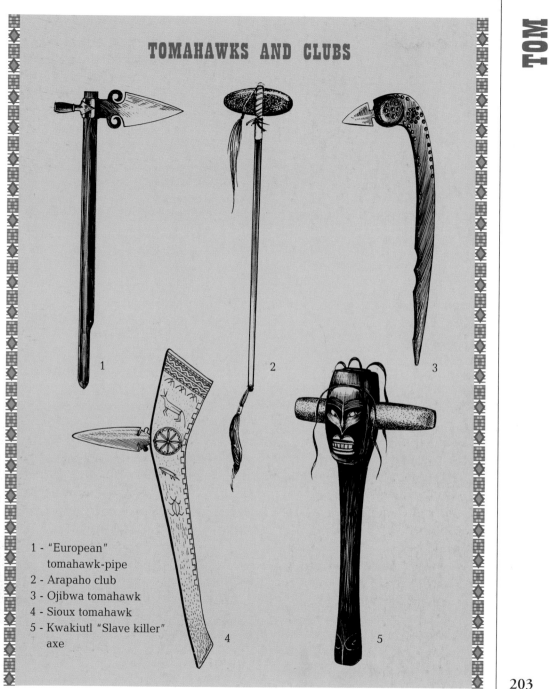

1 - "European" tomahawk-pipe
2 - Arapaho club
3 - Ojibwa tomahawk
4 - Sioux tomahawk
5 - Kwakiutl "Slave killer" axe

- Their few descendants occupy a reservation in Oklahoma: 1,500 in 1690, and 56 in 1944.

Totem

A term that came from *ototeman*, meaning "he is of my blood" in Chippewa and other dialects of the Algonquian family. This meaning leads to the idea that the totem, generally an animal, is the common ancestor of the animals of his species and the men of the clan who identify with it; for them, he is the protector, the dominant SPIRIT. This relationship entails certain constraints: a man of the Bear clan can only marry a woman of another clan; the hunters of the Deer clan may not kill this animal and thus procure its flesh or hide from hunters of another clan. There is a desire to demonstrate the qualities of the totem animal: the SNAKE's patience and prudence, the deer's speed, the BEAR's force, and more. Certain peoples of the Northwest (Haida, Kwakiutl) erected large wooden posts, or totem poles, in their villages. Generally made from the trunk of a thuja or sequoia tree measuring 16 to 20 feet (5 to 6 meters) in height, skillfully sculpted and painted in bright colors, totem poles told the story of a family or a clan and highlighted the protector animal that was associated with them.

Haida totem

Trade

Within the framework of peaceful relations, the use of "gifts" was common among the Indians, but the idea of actually trading was only successful when aimed at acquiring previously unknown goods, which were, therefore, attractive by definition. On the Great Plains, in the spring, there were organized gatherings among the tribes, permitting profitable exchanges such as agricultural products for furs, tobacco for seashells, sheets of copper or any other product that came from faraway places through successive trades.

A Cheyenne or an Arapaho might, for example, have had a bone BOW and not have been aware of its origins. This bow might have been acquired in exchange with a Blackfoot, who would have traded it for a bison hide with a Chinook who in turn received it from a Salish from the Pacific coast, because the bone was, in fact, baleen.

Traditionally, the SALISH from the coast traded with those with whom they had language in common, but who lived in the interior regions. The most active of the intermediaries were the CHINOOK, a network of small autonomous tribes spread throughout the lower Columbia. A link between two different regions, the Chinook focused on two activities: fishing salmon and trade. They managed the trade of furs, dried fish, fish oil, seashells, baskets, and, also, slaves.

Rendezvous points were near the confluence of the Columbia and Deschutes Rivers. The negotiations were conducted in a composite language, a combination of Salish, Chinook, and Nootka. This language was called "Chinook" and integrated French and English words when the whites became active in these trading activities at the beginning of the nineteenth century.

More toward the east, the Ojibwa traded their surplus of wild rice or corn for furs from the Cree or the Chipewyan. The Ojibwa and the Ottawa, found at the edges of the Great Plains, participated in north–south trade for agricultural products, pottery and,

especially, tobacco, which was used, but not produced, in the north. The arrival of the whites intensified the fur trade. The Iroquois and the Algonquin were rivals for beaver fur, at the risk of the species' survival; later, the appeal of bison hide would, in turn, lead to the disappearance of the vast herd that had lived on the Great Plains. Commerce had other consequences when the whites offered guns, gun powder, and alcohol as trade currency.

Trail of Tears

This is the name given to the forced displacement of 15,000 CHEROKEE who, in the spring of 1838, were made to leave their ancestral lands along the banks of the Mississippi for territories in OKLAHOMA. During this long journey, more than a third of the Cherokee nation was lost in conditions of extreme cold and famine.

Travois

As Indians did not use the wheel, they built travois with two long poles attached together, which made it possible to transport the heaviest loads: dismantled tipis, clothing, blankets, small children, and older people. The ends of the poles dragged on the ground and an animal skin was stretched over the middle, forming a stretcher-like structure. At first pulled by DOGS, HORSES were used for this after that animal became part of the lives of Indians.

Treaties

Without going back to agreements signed before American independence, the conquest of Indian territories during the eighteenth and nineteenth centuries was punctuated by treaties signed between the authorities (English, American, or Canadian) and the tribes. From the treaty of September 17, 1778, with the Delaware until 1871, the date on which Congress discontinued its policy of treaties with the tribes, more than 700 treaties and revisions were signed. The most notable were the New Echota treaty (1835) a prelude to the exile of the Cherokee on the TRAIL OF TEARS, the two Fort Laramie treaties (1851 and 1868), and the Medicine Lodge treaty (1867) with the Plains tribes. Almost universally, these commitments were not upheld by the whites either in their form or their substance.

Tribe

The family is the basic unit of the Indian community. It may be composed using male lineage, but most often female lineage, and the family includes, in a broader sense than in European societies, all individuals who are related by blood. Each person has his or her specific role to assume in the family unit, and a set of customs governs life and relationships between the family's various members; from the use of jokes, which is forbidden to various people: to not look such or such a person in the eyes, to not eat in that person's presence, to not say the person's name, to only speak to the person via the intermediary of a third party. The terms father, mother, son, sister, and the like were used without there necessarily being family relationships: thus the Indians called the president of the United States "father," and the word "child" could signify a dependent relationship with respect to another person. Many families claiming a common ancestor could come together and form a clan.

Each clan was placed under the protection of a totem animal or object: wolf, eagle, arrow, bear, deer, wind, and so on. The TOTEM was not the object of worship, but a spiritual guide for the clan, implying various taboos; if the totem was a bird, it was forbidden to kill it, eat its flesh, or wear its feathers. The life of the totem animal inspired songs and dances by the clan members.

Many clans constituted a brotherhood, and many brotherhoods constituted a half-tribe. While the brotherhood system bringing many families together was applied in ancient Greece, the subdivision into two halves is an Indian invention: this might seem to be a useless complication, but its value was in the distribution of responsibilities and POWERS.

Tsimshian

• Name meant: "people of the Skeena River."
• Language: Penutian.
• Settled in the estuary of the Skeena River, in large villages of plank houses.
• They fished (salmon) and hunted (bear, deer). Tightly linked to the HAIDA and the TLINGIT, they are much less warlike. The Tsimshian were adept at sculpting wood, bone, and ivory. The society obeyed a rigid hierarchy, from the hereditary aristocracy to the slaves. Social customs were elaborate, and art was sophisticated, thanks to the level of comfort that was enabled by the exceptional riches of the ocean and rivers.
• Each family or lineage had its particular emblem (TOTEM), representing the

animal or supernatural being that was supposed to have created it. This emblem was found everywhere: on poles in front of houses, on TATTOOS, embroideries, masks, canoes, and so on.
• Had only rare contact with the white world until the arrival of the Hudson Bay Company (1831). The Tsimshian then were subjected to the pressure of fur merchants, GOLD seekers, and other prospectors.
• Population estimated at 5,000 individuals at the beginning of the nineteenth century. They numbered 1,700 in 1968.

207

Tundra

Northern zone of the American continent, subject to arctic cold. The only vegetation growing there is limited to some dwarf willows, silver birch, mosses, and lichens.

Turkey

(*Meleagris gallopavo*). Wild turkeys lived throughout the entire southeast. For the Indians, they were an abundant source of game, but some tribes saw turkeys as stupid and fearful, so would not eat them for fear of inheriting their flaws!

Turquoise

A precious stone, the color of which varies from blue to blue-green. Mines were operated before the arrival of whites, in the present-day states of Colorado, New Mexico, Utah, Nevada, and California. The Pueblo, Zuni, and Navajo Indians specialized in creating jewelry from turquoise.

Tuscarora

• A corruption of their name for themselves, *Ska-ru-re*, meaning "those who gather hemp."
• Language: Iroquoian.
• Lived in the northeastern part of North Carolina, bordering the coast.
• They saw the whites arrive in 1508, and disputes quickly arose; the Tuscarora were defeated and migrated toward the north to join with the IROQUOIS, south of Lake Ontario, thus becoming the sixth component of the League (1722). In 1846 they were moved to Indian territory.
• There were 5,000 in 1600 and 793 in 1985 in the Tuscarora reservation (New York state). (*See* also Iroquois.)

Tutchone

• Means "crow people." Also called Caribou Indians and Wood Indians by fur traders.
• Language: Athabascan.
• Lived in the southern part of the Yukon.
• There were 1,000 in 1910. They have since probably integrated into other tribes.

Tutelo

• Meaning unknown. Were also called *Tuteras*.
• Language: Siouan.
• Lived in the region around the city of Roanoke, Virginia.
• Migrated toward the north and progressively integrated with the Cayuga, despite language differences.
• With other small Siouan-language tribes, they numbered 750 in 1701. The last Tutelo died in 1871.

U-V

Umatilla

- Meaning unknown.
- Language: Shahaptian.
- Settled at the confluence of the Umatilla and Columbia Rivers in northern Oregon. They were neighbors of the Cayuse, Walla Walla, and the Nez Perce.
- Visited by the LEWIS and CLARK expedition in 1806.
- Survived thanks to gathering, hunting, and fishing (salmon, mussels).
- They numbered 1,500 in 1780, but there are approximately 2,000 today on a reservation shared with the Cayuse and the Walla Walla.

Umiak

See Boats.

Ute

- Their name and all of its variants (*Uta, Utaw, Utsia, Youtah*) might be a corruption of their own name *Notch* (meaning "unknown"). Certain tribes called them "Black men" or "Black people."
- Language: Shoshonean.
- The Eastern Ute lived in central and western Colorado; the Western Ute lived in eastern Utah.
- The Ute were BISON hunters,

and were also known for their talents as dancers. Their ceremonies attracted tribes from the entire region.

• They were a people reputed to be aggressive, closely linked with the SHOSHONE and the BANNOCK. They responded to the white invasion by stealing livestock and horses. They fought with determination against the settlement of Mormons in the valley of the Great Salt Lake (1855). Under the influence of chief Ouray, their relationships with the whites progressively became more peaceful, aside from a revolt in 1879.

• Numbers estimated at 4,500 in 1845; they numbered 2,163 in 1937, and 4,700 in 1985.

Vancouver
George (1757-1798)

An English navigator, he took part in Cook's second and third voyages. After becoming a commander, he was sent to take possession of Nootka Bay for Great Britain, and to explore the northwest coast of America. For 3 years he made detailed maps of the coast, and of the island that bears his name.

Vasquez de Ayllon
Lucas (?-1528)

A conquistador and native of Toledo, Spain, he took part in an expedition to South Carolina in 1521 to procure slaves, but the plans were cut short due to the wreck of one of the two ships. Undaunted, he returned in 1526 to found a colony and resume his search for slaves, but the Indians massacred most of the Spanish, and Ayllon succumbed to his wounds upon his return to Santo Domingo.

Vespucci
Amerigo (1451-1519)

A navigator from Florence, Italy, he made four voyages to the west, and probably explored the coasts of South America as far as the mouth of the Amazon in 1500. *See* Waldseemüller.

Vikings

In the tenth century, the Celts and Vikings established colonies on the coasts of Greenland. While navigating his drakkar, or longship, through these waters in search of plunder, Erik the Red settled in Brattahlidh (the present-day city of Julianenhab). In search of wood, Erik decided to push toward the west; with his companions, he reached Baffin, and from there, in 984, they brought back not wood, but walrus ivory, animal oil, skins, and leather. Bjarni Herjolfsson, another Viking trying to rejoin his father, who was Erik's companion, got lost in a storm, headed south in his drakkar and saw a piece of land covered with forests. Believing in Bjarni's story, Erik's son Leif Eriksson decided to search for this land and after 5 days at sea, landed in northern Newfoundland, which he named Vinland, in the year 1000. Newfoundland was for many years the object of other voyages: The first was led by Erik the

Red's second son Thorvald; a subsequent one was led by Thorfinnr Karlsefni, who founded a colony, L'Anse aux Meadows, which could not survive due to the hostility of the Beotuk Indians, whom the Vikings nicknamed the *Skraelingjars*, "the ugly men." Because they were settled there, the Vikings made regular forays on the coasts of Labrador (Markland, "land of forests"). They had set foot on the American continent almost five centuries before Christopher Columbus, who, having traveled to Iceland before his American expedition, may have benefited from certain pieces of information.

Vision

According great importance to his dreams, which he interpreted as premonitions, an Indian sought out this state. The practice of prolonged sweating was popular throughout the Plains and Great Lakes tribes. Sweat sessions took place in shelters (*onikaghe* or sweat lodges) which were reserved for this use. Sweating, immobile, and deprived of food, the Indian waited for the moment when, on the brink of fainting, he would have hallucinations at the end of this purification. The interpretation of these visions would affect decisions that could be vital for him and his tribe: wars, hunts, the migration of the village, and more.

W

Wabash

A devastating battle that took place on November 4, 1791, on the banks of the Wabash River (the present-day border between Indiana and Illinois). The young American nation wanted to be done with the tribes that had supported the English during the American War of Independence; the Indians, on the contrary, were claiming their independence. The conflict turned into a resounding defeat for the Americans, led by General Arthur St. Clair, against the Indians of LITTLE TURTLE, chief of the Miami, who led a vast coalition of Mohawk, Shawnee, Delaware, Chippewa, Cherokee, Creek, and Osage warriors.

Wahpekute

Name means "those who tap their feet in the leaves." A division of the Santee. *See* Dakota.

Wahpeton

Name means "those who live among the leaves." A division of the Santee. *See* Dakota.

Walapai

- From *Xawalapaiy*, "those of the pine."
- Language: Yuman.
- Lived along the middle part of the Colorado River in northern Arizona.
- In the nineteenth century, they opposed the white invasion by ranchers and gold seekers. They were among the tribes who supported the GHOST DANCE worship.
- Numbered 7,000 in 1680 and 454 in 1937.

Waldseemüller
Martin (1480-1521)

A German geographer and cartographer born in Fribourg, also known by the Latin name *Hylacomilus*. He lived and died in Alsace. He is the author of the first map (1507) to include, in the form of a narrow band of land, what he called "Americi Terra del America," from the name of Amerigo Vespucci, to whom he attributed the discovery of this new land. Waldseemüller would later correct his error by attributing to Columbus what was his, but the name America had already stuck.

houses were grouped into villages, protected by a fence.
• They were farmers, small game hunters, and fishermen.
• Their chief MASSASSOIT came to the aid of the pilgrims from the *Mayflower* in 1620, and taught them to grow corn. The settlement of the colonists took place to the detriment of other tribes such as the Pequot.

Walla Walla
• Their name means "small river."
• Language: Shahaptian/Penutian.
• Settled along the lower part of the Walla Walla River (southeastern Washington and northeastern Oregon).
• Traditional fishing-based culture.
• Participated in the fight of the Plateau tribes, from 1853 to 1858.
• Their descendants settled on the Umatilla reservation (Oregon). Population estimated at 1,500 in 1780; they numbered 631 in 1937.

Wampanoag
• Name means "people of the east."
• Language: Algonquian.
• Lived in the present-day state of Massachusetts. Their small round

• Massassoit died in 1662. His oldest son METACOM, whom the whites nicknamed King Philip, succeeded him. In 1675 and 1676, he carried out a bloody war against the colonists and their allies the Mohegans. He was killed in 1676, and his nation was defeated. Survivors were sold as slaves.

• There were 2,400 Wampanoag in 1600 and 400 in 1700, integrated into neighboring tribes. Today, approximately 400 descendants live on the Wampanoag Reservation on Martha's Vineyard, Massachusetts, directed by a tribal counsel.

Wampum

To celebrate an event or record the terms of a treaty, the Algonquin and Iroquois Indians made wampums (a contraction of the Algonquin word *wampumpeag*), a composition of fragments of cylindrical stones threaded like pearls on a necklace, and assembled into the form of a sash or belt. Wampums were greatly valued and

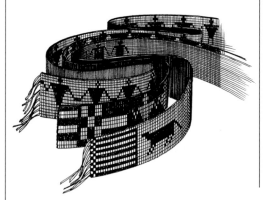

were endowed with soothing powers during mourning and condolence rituals. Wampums also served as an exchange currency between tribes and colonists.

Wapiti

The name of this type of elk means "white rump." Aside from some locations in southern Canada and the Ohio Valley, the wapiti (*Cervus elaphus*) primarily lives in the Rockies and in California. A close relative of the European deer, this was the game animal of choice for the Indians (certain males reached over 1,000 pounds/500 kilograms). Its brown fur was made into jackets and coats. Its horns supplied the HUPA with the primary material to make spoons, the use of which was essentially restricted to men.

Wappo

- Corruption of the Spanish word *guapo*, "brave/honest."
- Language: Yukian.
- Lived in the valley of the Russian and Naja Rivers, north of present-day San Francisco.
- Their resistance to Spanish invasion earned them their name.
- They numbered 10,000 in 1770 and 73 in 1910.

Wasco

- Meaning unknown.
- Language: Chinookan.
- Lived along the Columbia River, near the present-day city of Dallas.
- They numbered 900 in 1822 and 227 in 1937.

Washakie

(circa 1814-1900)

A great war chief, he unified the SHOSHONE and fought energetically against the hostile tribes (Sioux and Cheyenne). Persuaded that his people's survival depended on an agreement with the whites, he increased the number of concessions and facilitated the passage of the railroad through Indian lands. A friend of Kit CARSON and John FRÉMONT, he spoke English, French, and many Indian dialects. Washakie assisted the U.S. Army in its fight against the Blackfeet, the Crow, and the Dakota and obtained the large Wind River reservation for the Shoshone. At the battle of ROSEBUD (1876), he saved General Crook from disaster.

Washington
George (1732-1799)

The emblematic commander of the fight for American independence. He defeated the English at Yorktown (1781) with the assistance of La Fayette and Rochambeau. He had the Constitution voted on in 1787 and was twice elected president of the Union, in 1789 and 1792. He refused a third term.

Washita

On the Washita River, a pitiful victory of CUSTER's seventh cavalry regiment on November 27, 1868. 105 Cheyenne men, women and children, including their chief Black Kettle, were massacred at dawn. In accordance with General SHERIDAN's instructions, the 800 horses raised by the tribe were also slaughtered.

Washo

- From *Washiu*, "person."
- Language: Hokan.
- Settled in western Nevada.
- Known for their skills as basket weavers.
- Defeated by the PAIUTE who pushed them back toward the area of Reno (1862). The government offered them two reservations, which the white colonists occupied even before the Washo settled there (1865).
- There were approximately 1,000 individuals in 1845; they numbered 600 in 1937 and 666 in 1985.

Wea
See Miami.

Wenatchee
- Means "those of the river which comes from the canyon."
- Language: Salishan.
- Lived along the Wenatchee River and the lake of the same name, in central Washington state.
- They numbered 1,400 in 1780 and 52 in 1910.

Western Apache
See Apache.

Whales

Certain Pacific coast tribes used cetaceans (right whales, humpback whales, gray whales, blue whales, as well as orcas—which kill whales) as a principal source of subsistence. Daring fishermen from the NOOTKA and MAKAH tribes would pursue them on the open seas. Other tribes (Haida, Tlingit, Tsimishan, and Chumash in Southern California) were more cautious and waited until a whale would wash up on the shore.

White-tailed deer

Name given by Georges Louis Leclerc de Buffon to what is also called the Virginia deer (*Odocoileus virginiamus*). When danger strikes, the deer lifts its tail and a tuft of white fur is exposed, alerting the animal's fellow creatures.

Wichita

• According to sources, their name comes from *Wits*, "men," or from the Choctaw word *Wiachitoh*, "large tree" (an allusion to their dwellings). They gave themselves the name *Kirikitish*, (undoubtedly "the true men").
• Language: Caddoan.
• Lived in the Wichita Mountains in Oklahoma.
• The Wichita came from the south and farmed corn, squash, and TOBACCO, which they traded with other tribes. They became BISON hunters. Honest and hospitable, they were sensitive to the smallest insult.
• The Wichita were in Kansas when Coronado encountered them in 1541. Their first treaty was in 1835 with the federal government. They lived in Oklahoma until the beginning of

White Buffalo Cow Society

A SOCIETY organized by women, common to the Mandan and Hidatsa tribes, the goal of which was to incite, through their dances, tribes of bison to come near their villages.

White Mountain Apache

See Apache.

the Civil War, then were displaced to Kansas. In 1867 they definitively returned to Oklahoma on the Caddo reservation.
• They numbered 3,200 in 1780 and 460 in 1970.

Wigwam

For the forest Indians, this term meant "dwelling" and denoted conical or dome-shaped shelters, whatever the material used (birch bark, rushes, caribou skin, etc.). This name was used by travelers to designate Indian dwellings in general; it also took on the meaning of "household."

Winnebago

• From the Algonquin word *Winipyagohagi*, "people of the stagnant water." They called themselves *Hochangara*, "people of the true word," an allusion to their belief that they constituted one of the mother tribes of the Sioux.
• Language: Siouan.
• Settled north of the western bank of Lake Michigan (Door peninsula and Green Bay).

• They were BISON hunters and grew corn, tobacco, beans, and squash. Very hospitable, they were close to the DAKOTA in their customs and beliefs.
• Allies of the French and then the English, the Winnebago opposed the Americans until the end of BLACK HAWK's revolt (1832). They were almost annihilated by epidemics.
• RESERVATIONS in Nebraska (4,200 individuals in 1990) and Wisconsin, shared with the Omaha (5,000). Like numerous other Indian peoples, the Winnebago are deploying great efforts to reclaim their objects, decorative clothing, and other archaeological traces that are in American museums.

Wintun

- Means "people."
- Language: Penutian.
- Lived on the western side of the valley of the Sacramento River, between the cities of Red Bluff to the north and Princeton to the south.
- There were 12,000 in 1770, 512 in 1930, and 355 in 1985.

Wolf

The wolf (*Canis lupus*) was found throughout all of northern North America. An intelligent and social animal, wolves lived and hunted in packs of five to seven, and sometimes up to fifteen animals. Although they competed with Indian hunters for prey, it was a taboo animal for most of the Athabascans and especially for the Chipewyan who saw it as being similar to the dog, which was itself man's brother.

Women

An Indian woman takes on a large number of tasks, but her role and her prerogatives vary according to tribes and cultures. Sometimes she is only a slave, crushed by work, and expected most of all to bring a maximum number of children into the world. Fortunately, she isn't always confined to a subordinate role, and her place within the FAMILY and thus within the tribe, is sometimes a major one. Thus, IROQUOIS women have real power, participating in the

selection of chiefs and in their eviction if they perform poorly. In the majority of tribes, women hold economic power: the dwelling and all of the possessions belong to them, as well as sometimes the harvests, horses, and other household animals.

In a general way, women are responsible for the work related to the upkeep of the household, preparation of food, and the sewing of clothes, bags and moccasins. They are expert at tanning and preparing animal skins, spinning animal wool, and weaving and BASKET WEAVING. In farming tribes, the women do their part of the field work: the men clear and prepare the ground, the

Apaches

Dakota

Cheyenne

women plant and harvest (corn, beans, potatoes, tomatoes, etc.). Likewise, while jewelry making and pottery are mostly men's work, women prepare decorations made of feathers, porcupine spines, seeds and shells to adorn clothing, headdresses, bags and other accessories. Beginning in the eighteenth century, the arrival of colored pearls, obtained in trades with the whites, changed this traditional artistry, in particular for the making of WAMPUM.

It is difficult to know if Indian women spent much time cooking, but on the other hand it is certain that drying meat (jerky) or fish and preparing PEMMICAN were long and detailed procedures.

Women's National Indian Association

A feminist movement, which was very active in defending the rights of Indian tribes: the movement's reference book was Helen Hunt Jackson's work "*A Century of Dishonor*," published in 1881.

Wounded Knee

The death of SITTING BULL, on December 15, 1890, plunged the Sioux into despair, but many of them firmly believed that, according to the promise of the *messiah* WOVOKA, the whites would soon depart and the bison and warriors killed in combat would return. On December 29, 1890, the army intercepted a band of 350 Indians (120 warriors, 230 women and children), who, under the direction of chief BIG FOOT, were attempting to return to the Pine Ridge reservation. Colonel Forsyth, who commanded the seventh cavalry regiment, led the Indians to Wounded Knee to disarm them. An incident occurred, and the Indians, convinced that they were protected from bullets by their "sacred shirts," revolted. Battle was engaged, resulting in the death of 250 Indians, most of them killed by machine gun fire in a few minutes. The tragedy at Wounded Knee marked the end of the GHOST DANCE and put an end to the Indian revolts.

In 1973, militants from the American Indian Movement occupied the site of Wounded Knee in order to evoke the past and present situations of the Indians. Repression was very strict and resulted in high levels of tension on Indian reservations until 1975.

Wovoka
(1856-circa 1930)

A Paiute medicine man, founder of the GHOST DANCE movement. Born in Nevada, he was raised, after his father's death, in a family of white ranchers who named him Jack Wilson. In about 1880, he began to spread prophecies heralding a "new age," in which the whites and epidemics would disappear, the Indians would find abundant lands, and the bison would return.

The Ghost Dance found numerous disciples among the Plains Indians, who adapted the essence of its message to their aspirations, writing their own songs and creating their own dances. In 1889 a delegation of Dakota Sioux visited Wovoka. It brought back "sacred shirts" to the reservation, which were supposed to be bulletproof. Alas, the massacre at WOUNDED KNEE (1890) rapidly proved that the New Age would not come. Wovoka rapidly lost his notoriety and resumed using the name Jack Wilson until his death in the 1930s.

Wyandot
See Huron.

Y-Z

Yahi and Yana

The Yahi were integrated by the Yana.
- Both names mean "person" in their common language.
- Language: Hokan.
- They lived along the upper part of the Sacramento River.
- Together they numbered 1,500 in 1770 and 9 in 1930.

Yakima

- Their name means "fugitives." They called themselves *Waptailmin*, "people of the narrow river."
- Language: Shahaptian/Penutian.
- They settled along the lower part of the Yakima River (Washington state), not far from the present-day city of Seattle.
- They were traditionally fishermen and hunters, with their activities varying depending on seasonal migrations. From the beginning of May until the end of July, SALMON fishing in the waters of the Columbia represented the bountiful time of year. Closely related to the NEZ PERCE, they also hunted BISON.

- Encountered by LEWIS and CLARK in 1805. Like their neighbors, the Yakima opposed the invasion of their lands by GOLD seekers and fought from 1853 to 1859, under the direction of their chief Kamaikin. Defeated, they submitted to the Fort Elliot treaty and moved to a RESERVATION in Washington state.
- There were 3,000 in 1780. They shared their reservation with the Klickitat, Palouse, and Wasco; census numbers reflect the total population on the reservation: 4,500 in 1914, 5,391 in 1970, and 8,500 in 1990. Very well organized, they have tribal schools, police, and courts of justice. They changed their name to Yakama (1994).

Yamassee

- Means "kind."
- Language: Muskogean.
- They lived along the Ocmulgee River in southeastern Georgia.
- The invasion of their lands by the Spanish and English caused the Yamassee to revolt in 1715. They killed 90 colonists and their families. The reaction of the colonists pushed the Yamassee to the south, toward Florida, where they integrated with the SEMINOLE.
- There were 2,000 in 1650. Their few descendants are impossible to count.

Yankton

- The name means "end of the village."
- Together with the Yanktonai, they compose the Nakota division of the

DAKOTA nation (whose language they share, but with different pronunciation).

Yavapais

- Means "people of the sun."
- Language: Yuman.
- Western Arizona was home to the Yavapai.
- They numbered 600 in 1680 and 194 in 1934.

Yellowknives

• Their true name, *Tatsanottine*, meant "men of the scum water." Better known by the names Copper Indians, Yellow Knives, or Red Knives, names that referred to the ore in the Coppermine River.

• Language: Athabascan.

• Lived on the northern and eastern banks of the Great Slave Lake.

• Hunted CARIBOU and musk ox on the Canadian taiga. They were very strict in educating their young for combat and hunting. The children had to swim in icy water, sleep naked outside in the cold, fast for days, and run long distances.

• The history of the Tatsanottine is copper-colored. They were rich in this ore, which enabled the production of weapons and tools, and they benefited from a privileged and affluent lifestyle. However, when the Europeans introduced items made of iron and steel, the Yellowknives were powerless before this competition and slowly migrated south.

• Their numbers were estimated at 500 in 1906 and about 1,000 today.

Yokut

• The names means "men" in their own dialect. They are also called the *Mariposans*.

• Language: Related to Penutian.

• Settled in the San Joaquin Valley (California).

• Hunters and farmers.

• Many of them escaped the Spanish MISSIONS but were victims of American expansion following the GOLD rush (1849).

• They may have numbered 18,000 in 1770; there were approximately 1,000 in 1930 and 504 in 1970.

Yuchi

• The names means "those who come from afar." Their name for themselves, *Tsoyama*, means "men of the sun."

• Language: Siouan.

counted 1,216 descendants of the Yuchi, of which about half are of mixed race.

Yuki

• The name means "stranger" or "enemy."
• Language: Yukian.
• They lived in northwestern California, in the same location as their Round Valley reservation.
• They numbered 2,000 in 1770 and 177 in 1930 combined with the Huchnoms.

Yukon

Canadian region west of the Northwest Territories, bounded by the Alaskan border and, to the south, by British Columbia. The Yukon underwent an upheaval after the discovery of gold in the KLONDIKE Valley in 1826. Dawson, at the confluence of the Yukon and Klondike Rivers, was the point of convergence for thousands of gold seekers. The life of some Indian tribes who lived in these immense forests was forever disrupted.

Yuma

• Spanish contraction of *Yahmayo*, "the chief's son," the title of the person who inherited power in the tribe. They called themselves *Kwichana*, or Quechans.
• Language: Yuman, associated with the Hokan linguistic family.

• Settled in eastern Tennessee.
• Living in a region of small mountains, they were independent and fierce warriors.
• In 1567, the Spanish inflicted heavy losses on them. In the face of pressure from colonists, they migrated toward the lands of the CREEK (1729), and some Yuchi followed the Creek to Oklahoma. Others increased the ranks of the SEMINOLE.
• Population estimated at 5,000 in the sixteenth century. The 1949 census

• Population estimated at 3,000 in 1776; the Yuma probably still number about the same, half of them in the Colorado River valley. The other half lives on the Yuma reservation in California.

Yurok

• From *Yuruk*, a Karok term meaning "downstream"; *Karuk* meant "upstream."
• Language: associated with Algonquian.

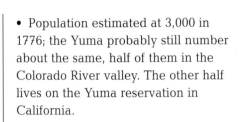

• They lived along the lower part of the Colorado River, near the confluence with the Gila.
• Possessing a natural elegance, the Yuma were feared warriors. Hunters and fishermen, they were also good farmers who practiced irrigation.
• Encountered by Hernando de Alarcon in 1540, they were in contact with other Spanish explorers and traders from the beginning of the eighteenth century. They granted the majority of their territory to the U.S. in the Treaty of Guadalupe Hidalgo in 1848.

226

- Lived along the lower part of the Klamath River in northern California.
- They were gatherers and fishermen known for their peaceful temperament. They were skilled artisans (basket weaving, wood sculpture).
- Late in entering into contact with the whites, they had minor conflicts with colonists and gold seekers. They were then spared thanks to the establishment of their territory as a RESERVATION in 1855, which is today connected with the Hupa reservation.
- May have numbered 2,500 in the nineteenth century. There were approximately 1,000 in 1985.

Zuni

- Spanish deformation of *Keresan Suni-yitsi*, the meaning of which is unknown. They called themselves *Ashiwi*, "the flesh."
- Language: Zunian, associated with Aztec-Tanoan.
- A PUEBLO people who lived on the north bank of the upper part of the Zuni River, a tributary of the Little Colorado River in northwestern New Mexico.
- A people of farmers and POTTERY experts, the Zuni, like the HOPI, practiced KACHINA worship. Four levels organized the society: the priests, responsible for interceding with the forces of the afterlife to bring rain, were at the summit of this hierarchy.
- The Zuni called their land *Shiwona* (or *Shiwinakwin*, "the land that produces flesh"). They participated in the revolt of 1680 and after this war were gathered on the site of present-day Zuni.
- Numbering 2,500 in 1680, the Zuni today number more than 10,000, settled on a RESERVATION in New Mexico. They have their own government (schools, police, court of justice) and have kept their language, traditions and some of the ancestral ceremonies (such as the Shalako, for the winter solstice) alive.

CHRONOLOGY

Between 40,000 and 30,000 B.C. First passages from Asia to Alaska using the Bering Strait. A second wave of passages took place between 25,000 and 10,000 B.C.

Circa 1000 Leif Eriksson lands in northern Newfoundland. The Vikings found a colony in L'Anse aux Meadows.

1492-1493 Christopher Columbus's first voyage. By 1504 he accomplished three other expeditions to the "West Indies."

1499-1500 Voyage of Amerigo Vespucci.

1513 Foray into Florida by Ponce de Leon. Fifteen years later, his countryman Pamfilo de Narvaez travels up the coasts of Florida as far as the mouth of the Mississippi.

1534 Jacques Cartier, sent by Francis I, drops anchor in the Saint Lawrence estuary. He takes possession of the territory in the name of the king of France and settles in the Indian village of Hochlaga, on the future site of Montreal.

1539-1543 The Spaniards Hernando de Soto and Francisco de Coronado pursue exploration of the southern United States. Coronado travels throughout the Pueblo region.

1541 After having been favorably welcomed, Jacques Cartier opposes the Iroquois, who force the French to leave by boat.

1562 and 1564 Two expeditions of French Protestants are sent by Admiral de Coligny with the goal of founding a colony in Florida.

1584 Sir Walter Raleigh takes possession, in the name of the English crown, of a territory that he names Virginia, in honor of his queen, Elizabeth. A colony is established on Roanoke island.

1603 Samuel de Champlain again begins exploring New France and travels up the Saint Lawrence as far as the Saint Louis drop.

1607 Three ships penetrate the Chesapeake Bay; they bring 105 English colonists who will found Jamestown. They designate Captain John Smith as their leader.

1608 Champlain founds Quebec on the site of the village of Stadoconé. He explores the length of the Saint Lawrence River as far as Lake Ontario, develops a fur trade and brings clergy to evangelize the Indians.

1620 Fleeing persecution in England, 102 members of a Protestant sect, the Puritans, land at Cape Code in their ship the *Mayflower*.

1626 Peter Minuit buys Manhattan Island from the Indians. There, his Dutch countrymen found New Amsterdam.

1629 Supporting the Protestants against Richelieu, the English are at war with France. They take Quebec, and the French must leave Canada.

1636 The English colonies of Massachusetts and Connecticut develop rapidly. The Puritans' fanaticism leads them to wage a war of extermination against the Indian tribes: In the name of God, savages, sons of the Devil, must be eliminated. The Pequot War ends in the extermination of this powerful tribe.

1643 So that Iroquois hunters will bring them more furs, the Dutch make the mistake of supplying muskets and ammunition to the Iroquois, who then threaten their neighboring tribes and then French establishments: farms, villages, cities. The war is intense until 1667.

1675 Metacom, whom the English mockingly call King Philip, becomes the chief of the Wampanoags. He leads a crusade to rally the tribes and expel the colonists. After a year of terrible fighting, Philip is killed. This defeat marks the end of the resistance of the New England tribes.

1681 Arrival of William Penn and the Quakers to a vast territory that will become Pennsylvania. The next year, Penn signs a friendship treaty with the Delaware.

1682 Leaving from Quebec, Jean Cavelier de La Salle reaches the mouth of the Mississippi: He takes possession of these territories and gives them the name Louisiana in honor of the king of France.

1684 Hostilities are reignited between the Iroquois and the French: The French, weakened by an incessant guerilla war, only control fortified locations such as Montreal in 1690.

1752 The French influence extends from Quebec to New Orleans via the Great Lakes and the valleys of the Illinois and Mississippi Rivers. The English have settled along the Atlantic coast, and their progress toward the west happens using coastal river valleys; the Hudson in the north, the Potomac toward the south. The French number 80,000 and the English, 1,500,000.

1756 In Europe, the Seven Years War begins. William Pitt, the head of the English government, is aware of the importance of the conflict in America and sends a powerful contingent. The French forts fall one by one. Quebec is under siege. Montcalm is killed and the city falls (1759). Montreal surrenders in 1760. France signs the Treaty of Paris on February 10, 1763. It loses Canada, the Ohio Valley, and the left bank of the Mississippi, keeping only Louisiana.

1763 Freed from French competition, nothing stops English expansion; this occurs to the detriment of the despised Indians. With the exception of some Iroquois who are faithful to their old allies, all the tribes rise up, motivated by the Ottawa chief Pontiac. The colonists are massacred, the soldiers abandon the forts, but the Indians are short on ammunition. Pontiac surrenders in 1766 and is assassinated in 1769.

1773 The rapid development of the colonies makes English oversight unbearable. The thirteen states rebel against the taxes imposed by London. On April 19, 1775, the conflict erupts near Boston. George Washington is named general in chief of the Union forces. Worried by the birth of this new state, the Indian tribes rally around England, their old enemy. But, financially and militarily supported by France, the American forces win at Saratoga in October 1777. After Cornwallis surrenders at Yorktown (1781), England agrees to end the war. The Treaty of Versailles preserves the United States' independence.

1782 Before the war has even ended, a federation of "United Indian Nations" is created. But the tribes are on the losers' side, and the colonists are unwilling to accept that the "savages" can exercise rights to the soil. Treaties are signed, and treaties are broken as soon as the ink has dried on the paper.

1790 The Indians cannot tolerate the settlement of colonists on a territory that they consider to be theirs. Led by chief Little Turtle, they begin hostilities and crush the Americans at the battle of Wabash (1791). General Wayne rectifies the situation. Signed by twelve tribes, the Greenville treaty (1795) is meant to establish a lasting agreement. The Indians lose more than half of the Ohio Valley but keep "forever" the lands to the west.

1804-1806 Launched upon President Jefferson's initiative, the Lewis and Clark expedition reaches the Pacific after crossing the Rocky Mountains and then comes back to the east.

1812 England has not given up on reclaiming its former colony. It arms and motivates the Indians, led by the Shawnee Tecumseh, to carry out raids on American establishment. The Union declares war on England. The Indians are divided, but the majority again backs the English. After a disastrous start, the Americans redouble their efforts at the Battle of the Thames, where Tecumseh is killed; they try to invade Canada, but the English avoid disaster thanks to their Indian allies.

1830 President Jackson has Congress adopt the Indian Renewal Act, which plans for the concentration of Indians in Oklahoma. The Huron, Shawnee, Miami, Delaware, Potawatonee, and Winnebago are forced into exile; to the south, the Cherokee, Creek, Choctaw, and Chickasaw suffer the same trial. None of the previous treaties is respected. Thousands of deaths mark the path into exile, the Trail of Tears (1838). This is one of the most tragic episodes of the Indian genocide.

1845-1848 Annexation by the United States of Texas, then of the entire southwest of the continent, at Mexico's expense. The Comanche and Apache retaliate with guerilla actions.

1848 Discovery of a gold deposit in California in Captain John Sutter's sawmill. This is the start of a human wave that will brutally oust the Indians summarily from the region.

1854 A minor incident (the Sioux appropriated a Mormon's lost cow) leads to a succession of killings. The Sioux, under the leadership of their greatest chiefs (Spotted Tail, Little Crow, Red Cloud, Crazy Horse, and Sitting Bull) begin a war which did not in fact end until 1890 at Wounded Knee. In 1868, the treaty of Fort Laramie satisfied the Sioux's requests regarding the bison hunt. This Indian victory was followed by several years of peace.

1858 Beginning of the final phase of the Apache wars, in which Cochise, killed in 1874, and Geronimo, who surrendered in 1886, distinguished themselves.

1861 The Civil War divides the states of the Union . . . and the Indians. Many opt for the south, but some tribes such as the Cherokee are tragically divided. Many Indians die in the battles, and the end of the war signals a new rush to the west.

1862-1875 The Great Plains bison are systematically exterminated, in particular during the construction of the transcontinental railroad.

1864 A group of peaceful Cheyenne put themselves under the protection of the star-covered flag near Fort Lyon, in a bend of the Sand Creek. A troop of 700 mounted troops under the leadership of General Chivington descends on the village, killing men, women, the elderly, and children. The Sand Creek Massacre seems to awaken the conscience of the Whites, many of whom declare their outrage.

1865 The government proposes the Washita peace treaty. The tribes agree to return to their reservations.

1865 General Sherman, leading the forces of the Mississippi, directs General Hannock to defeat the Dog Soldiers, an elite group of Cheyenne, Sioux, and Arapaho soldiers. They contest the treaties, launch independent actions, and threaten the construction of the transcontinental railroad. Thus begins a series of actions opposing the blue coats against the fiercest of the plains warriors. The Dog Soldiers are defeated in 1868, but the Kiowa and Comanche take over from them and continue the guerilla war until 1873.

1871 Congress abandons its policy of treaties. No Indian tribe or nation is recognized as an independent power.

1872 The government finishes constructing a railroad line between the Big Horn Mountains and the Black Hills. The construction of a fort

enables the discovery of a gold deposit, and then the rush of adventurers begins. The government wants to buy the region, but the Sioux chiefs refuse to sell their sacred mountain. General Crook is chosen to subdue the Indians. He is defeated at the Battle of Rosebud on June 17, 1876. One week later, Custer is crushed at Little Big Horn. The Sioux try to reach Canada but are mercilessly pursued.

1877 The war of the Nez Perce in Idaho and Montana ends in the final rendition of Chief Joseph.

1878-1879 The Cheyenne of chief Dull Knife have laid down their arms. They are forcibly driven to Oklahoma. In September, 300 of them head back to their lands. Despite difficulties and 2,000 people pursuing them, they arrive after 2 months of carnage. Decimated but victorious, the Cheyenne obtain a reservation in Bison country.

1887 The Dawes Act distributes tribal lands in parcels of 160 acres per family. This was meant to transform the Indians into small-scale landowners, but in fact the law allowed the dismantling of reservations and the repurchase of the land by white farmers at an attractive price.

1889 Breaking with its previous commitments and the solution imposed on the tribes in 1830 (Removal Act) and aiming to gather the Indians in Oklahoma territory, the Union government opens the borders of this state to white colonization.

1890 An air of mysticism blows over the Indian reservations, announcing the return of a messiah . . . an Indian! The Ghost Dance glorifies the spirits; the worried authorities send troops to the Sioux who are following the movement. Sitting Bull is killed. The tribes return to their reservations with the exception of a band of Hunkpapa Sioux who remain at Wounded Knee. A misunderstanding leads to a new massacre: more than 300 Indian men, women, and children are killed.

1924 By the Indian Citizenship Act, Indians born in the United States become full American citizens.

1928 Report of Lewis Meriam. For the first time, it is proposed to orient the policy toward Indians, taking into account the Indians' wishes as well as restitution for the wrongs caused.

1934 Within the framework of Franklin D. Roosevelt's New Deal, John Collier, the commissioner of the Bureau of Indian Affairs, proposes the Indian Reorganization Act, involving cultural and political reforms. The Indians will be consulted and invited to choose their society's system of organization: tribal government elected by majority or chosen by the elders.

1953 Under the Eisenhower administration, the House of Representatives passes Resolution 108, which discontinues federal responsibility for Indian Affairs. Presented as an act of liberation, the resolution is in fact a method for the government to exonerate itself from financial responsibility for Indian policy.

1961 Taking over the goals of the NCAI (National Congress of American Indians), young Indians form the NIYC (National Indian Youth Council) to make the voices of the poorest heard and to call on the authorities to ensure that certain historical rights are respected.

1968 Foundation of AIM (American Indian Movement), which is more demanding in its disputes.

1969 Occupation of Alcatraz Island in San Francisco Bay to raise American consciousness about the misery on reservations and the desire to maintain Indian traditions.

1973 Occupation of the historic site at Wounded Knee, South Dakota, to commemorate the massacre in 1890 and to denounce the ineffectiveness of the Bureau of Indian Affairs.

1978 The Indian "Long March," from San Francisco to Washington, is organized in the name of "Red Power" and its claims.

1983 With its Statement on Indian Policy, the Reagan administration confirms its liberal policy: elimination of administrative roadblocks and encouragement for the Indians to open their reservations to free enterprise and industrial investment. Happily, despite the difficulties of the journey, the Indians did not give up on making themselves heard in the United States and on the international scene. While the outcome of the reservations is still uncertain, the tragic history of the Indian people and the message that it brings us in its desire for survival invite us, in the face of environmental and wartime threats, to question ourselves as to our own future and that of the planet.

1990 The national census shows, for the United States, an Indian population of 1,878,000 individuals. The largest "native nations" are the Cherokee, Navajo, Chippewa (Ojibwa), Sioux, and Choctaw.